GW00693505

THE MAGNIFICENT JOURNEY

Being a Translation of

AR-RISĀLAT UT-TABŪKIYYAH

(THE MESSAGE FROM TABŪK)

بسم الله الرحمن الرحيم

THE MAGNIFICENT JOURNEY

Being a Translation of

AR-RISĀLAT UT-TABŪKIYYAH
(THE MESSAGE FROM TABŪK)

by

IBN QAYYIM IL-JAWZIYYAH

Translation and Comments
by
Muḥammad al-Jibālī

AL-QUR'ĀN WAS-SUNNAH SOCIETY
OF NORTH AMERICA

Copyright © 1995
by

Al-Qur'ān was-Sunnah Society of North America

ISBN 1-886451-00-1

All Rights Reserved

TABLE OF CONTENTS

PRELUDE

Introduction

Alḥamdu lillāh. Indeed, all glory and praise is due to Allāh. We glorify and praise Him and we ask Him for help and forgiveness. In Allāh we seek refuge from the evils of ourselves and from our wrong doings. He whom Allāh guides shall not be misguided, and he whom He misguides shall never be guided.

I bear witness that there is no [true] god except Allāh, alone without any partners, and I bear witness that Muḥammad (S) is His *'Abd* [1] and Messenger.

﴿يَا أَيُّهَا ٱلَّذِينَ آمَنُوا ٱتَّقُوا ٱللهَ حَقَّ تُقَاتِهِ وَلَا تَمُوتُنَّ إِلَّا وَأَنتُم مُّسْلِمُونَ﴾ آل عمران ١٠٢

«Believers! Fear and worship Allāh as He deserves, and do not die except as *Muslims*.» [2]

﴿يَا أَيُّهَا ٱلنَّاسُ ٱتَّقُوا رَبَّكُمُ ٱلَّذِي خَلَقَكُم مِّن نَّفْسٍ وَاحِدَةٍ، وَخَلَقَ مِنْهَا زَوْجَهَا، وَبَثَّ مِنْهُمَا رِجَالاً كَثِيراً وَنِسَاءً، وَٱتَّقُوا ٱللهَ ٱلَّذِي تَسَاءَلُونَ بِهِ وَٱلْأَرْحَامَ، إِنَّ ٱللهَ كَانَ عَلَيْكُمْ رَقِيباً﴾ النساء ١

«People! Be dutiful to your Lord who has created you from one soul, and created from it its mate, and from these two spread forth multitudes of men and women; and fear Allāh through whom you demand [your mutual rights], and [revere the ties of] the wombs. Indeed, Allāh is ever-watchful over you.» [3]

﴿يَا أَيُّهَا ٱلَّذِينَ آمَنُوا ٱتَّقُوا ٱللهَ وَقُولُوا قَوْلاً سَدِيداً، يُصْلِحْ لَكُمْ أَعْمَالَكُمْ، وَيَغْفِرْ لَكُمْ ذُنُوبَكُمْ، وَمَن يُطِعِ ٱللهَ وَرَسُولَهُ فَقَدْ فَازَ فَوْزاً عَظِيماً﴾ الأحزاب ٧٠-٧١

---

1 *'Abd*: Devoted servant and worshipper.

2 *Āl 'Imrān* 3:102.

3 *An-Nisā'* 4:1.

«Believers! Keep your duty to Allāh, and [always] speak the truth. He will then direct you to do righteous deeds and will forgive your sins. And whoever obeys Allāh and His Messenger has indeed achieved a great victory.» [1]

Verily, the best words are those of Allāh (T); the best guidance is that of Muḥammad (S); the worst matters [in creed or worship] are those innovated [by people], for every such innovated matter is a *bidʿah* [2], and every *bidʿah* is a misguidance which deserves the Fire. [3]

Our *Daʿwah* and Objectives

Our goal in this and in our other works is to attempt to implement and propagate the True *Daʿwah* [4] that we advocate. This *Daʿwah* derives from the Book of Allāh (T) and the *Sunnah* [5] of His Messenger (S), and is therefore our duty and the duty of every *Muslim*. Allāh (T) said:

﴿وَلْتَكُنْ مِنكُمْ أُمَّةٌ يَدْعُونَ إِلَى ٱلْخَيْرِ، وَيَأْمُرُونَ بِٱلْمَعْرُوفِ، وَيَنْهَوْنَ عَنِ ٱلْمُنْكَرِ، وَأُوْلَٰئِكَ هُمُ ٱلْمُفْلِحُونَ﴾ آل عمران ١٠٤

«Let there arise from you a group of people inviting to all that is good (*Islām*), enjoining what is right (according to *Islām*), and forbidding what is wrong (according to *Islām*). These are the ones who will achieve success.» [6]

The *Daʿwah* may be summarized in two words: *taṣfiyah* (cleansing and purification) and *tarbiyah* (cultivation and education). Allāh (T) refers to this in the following:

﴿هُوَ ٱلَّذِي بَعَثَ فِي ٱلْأُمِّيِّينَ رَسُولاً مِنْهُمْ يَتْلُو عَلَيْهِمْ آيَاتِهِ وَيُزَكِّيهِمْ وَيُعَلِّمُهُمُ ٱلْكِتَابَ وَٱلْحِكْمَةَ، وَإِنْ كَانُوا مِنْ قَبْلُ لَفِي ضَلَالٍ مُبِينٍ.﴾ الجمعة ٢

---

1 *Al-Aḥzāb* 33:70-71.

2 *Bidʿah*: Innovation in the creed or in acts of worship.

3 These opening paragraphs are a translation of *Khuṭbat ul-Ḥājah* (the Sermon of Need) with which the Messenger (S) used to start his speeches and which he was keen to teach to his companions.

4 *Daʿwah*: Call and mission.

5 *Sunnah*: Way.

6 *Āl ʿImrān* 3:104.

«He it is who has sent unto the unlettered people a Messenger from among themselves to convey unto them His messages, to purify them, and to teach them the Book and the Wisdom - whereas before that they had been, most obviously, lost in error.» [1]

To ensure success in pursuing our goal, we set the following objectives:

1. Return to the sublime *Qur'ān* and to the Prophet's authentic *Sunnah*, and comprehend them in accordance with the understanding and practice of the righteous *Salaf* (the *Ṣaḥābah* [2], may Allāh be pleased with them, and their true followers). This conforms with what Allāh (T) said:

   ﴿وَمَن يُشَاقِقِ ٱلرَّسُولَ مِنۢ بَعْدِ مَا تَبَيَّنَ لَهُ ٱلْهُدَىٰ، وَيَتَّبِعْ غَيْرَ سَبِيلِ ٱلْمُؤْمِنِينَ، نُوَلِّهِۦ مَا تَوَلَّىٰ، وَنُصْلِهِۦ جَهَنَّمَ، وَسَآءَتْ مَصِيرًا﴾ النساء ١١٥

   «If anyone contends with the Messenger even after the Guidance has been plainly conveyed to him, and follows a path other than that of the believers, We shall leave him in the path he has chosen, and land him in Hell: What an evil abode!» [3]

   And He said:

   ﴿فَإِنْ آمَنُوا بِمِثْلِ مَا آمَنتُم بِهِ فَقَدِ ٱهْتَدَوا﴾ البقرة ١٣٧

   «So if they believe as you believe [4], they are indeed on the right path.» [5]

2. Enlighten and educate *Muslims*, urging them to comply with the true *Dīn* [6], to act according to its teachings, and to adorn themselves with its virtues and ethics. This will ensure Allāh's acceptance, through which they will realize happiness and glory, as indicated in the following:

---

1 *Al-Jumu'ah* 62:2.

2 *Ṣaḥābah*: The Prophet's Companions.

3 *An-Nisā'* 4:115.

4 The address here is to the Companions of the Messenger (S).

5 *Al-Baqarah* 2:137.

6 *Dīn* : Religion.

﴿وَٱلْعَصْرِ، إِنَّ ٱلْإِنسَانَ لَفِي خُسْرٍ، إِلَّا ٱلَّذِينَ آمَنُوا وَعَمِلُوا ٱلصَّالِحَاتِ، وَتَوَاصَوْا بِٱلْحَقِّ وَتَوَاصَوْا بِٱلصَّبْرِ﴾ العصر ١-٣

«By the passing time, man is indeed in [a state of] loss, except those who attain to faith and do good deeds, and those who enjoin upon one another the keeping to truth, and enjoin upon one another patience in adversity.» [1]

3. Caution *Muslims* and exhort them to cleanse their lives of all forms of *shirk* (polytheism), *bidʿah*s, and philosophy or other thoughts alien to the pure, essential tenets of *Islām*. This is a duty that Allāh (T) enjoined on us by saying:

﴿وَتَعَاوَنُوا عَلَى ٱلْبِرِّ وَٱلتَّقْوَى، وَلَا تَعَاوَنُوا عَلَى ٱلْإِثْمِ وَٱلْعُدْوَانِ﴾ المائدة ٢

«Help you one another in righteousness and piety, but do not help one another in sinning and transgression.» [2]

4. Cleanse the *Sunnah* of the weak and fabricated narrations. The problems referred to in this and the previous objective have marred the clarity of *Islām* and have prevented the advancement of *Muslims*. This objective is of extreme vitality, and it furnishes us with an important resource, as the Messenger (S) said:

‹This knowledge will be carried by the trustworthy ones of every generation - they will expel from it the alterations made by those going beyond bounds, the false claims of the liars, and the false interpretations of the ignorant.› [3]

5. Strive to: revive unobstructed *Islām*ic thought within the boundaries of *Islām*ic principles [4], oppose stubborn adherence to *ma<u>th</u>hab*s [5],

---

1 *Al-ʿAṣr* 103:1-3.

2 *Al-Māʾidah* 5:2.

3 Authentic - Reported by Ibn ʿ*Adiyy and others.*

4 These principles are described in point "1" above.

5 *Ma<u>th</u>hab*: Way or approach. It mostly refers to one of the four *Islām*ic schools of legislation and jurisprudence that were based on the research and understanding of the Four *Imāms*: Abū Ḥanīfah an-Nuʿmān bin Thābit, Mālik bin Anas, Aḥmad bin Ḥanbal, and Muḥammad bin Idrīs ash-Shāfiʿī - May Allāh (T) bestow His mercy on them all.

and oppose prejudiced loyalty to parties. The problems indicated here have rested upon the minds of many *Muslims*, diverting them from the pure original sources of *Islām*, and causing them to deviate from the honest *Islām*ic brotherhood called to by Allāh (T):

﴿وَٱعْتَصِمُوا بِحَبْلِ ٱللهِ جَمِيعاً، وَلَا تَفَرَّقُوا﴾ آل عمران ١٠٣

«And hold fast all together, by the rope of Allāh, and be not divided among yourselves.» [1]

And by His Messenger (S):

‹Be, worshippers of Allāh, one brethren.› [2]

6. Present realistic *Islām*ic solutions to contemporary problems, and strive to resume a true *Islām*ic way of life and to establish a true *Islām*ic society governed by Allāh's law. Allāh (T) said:

﴿وَأَنِ ٱحْكُمْ بَيْنَهُمْ بِمَا أَنْزَلَ ٱللهُ وَلَا تَتَّبِعْ أَهْوَاءَهُمْ﴾ المائدة ٤٩

«Hence, judge between them in accordance with what Allāh has revealed, and do not follow their errant views.» [3]

We call upon all *Muslims* to support us in carrying out this noble trust which will elevate and honor them and spread the eternal message of *Islām* all over earth, as is Allāh's true promise:

﴿هُوَ ٱلَّذِي أَرْسَلَ رَسُولَهُ بِٱلْهُدَىٰ وَدِينِ ٱلْحَقِّ لِيُظْهِرَهُ عَلَى ٱلدِّينِ كُلِّهِ
وَلَوْ كَرِهَ ٱلْمُشْرِكُونَ﴾ الصف ٩

«He it is who has sent His Messenger with Guidance and the Religion of Truth, in order to make it prevail over all [false] religion, however hateful this may be to the *Mushrikīn* (those who ascribe divinity to other than Allāh).» [4]

General Approach in This Work

A large number of *Islām*ic writings in recent times lack the correctness

1 *Āl ʿImrān* 3:103.
2 Al-Bukhārī and Muslim.
3 *Al-Māʾidah* 5:49.
4 *Aṣ-Ṣaff* 61:9.

and preciseness of a true *Islām*ic approach. They suffer from two major problems:

1. Unconcern about the importance of relying only on authentic evidence, particularly in quoting *Ḥadīth* [1]. Thus some conclusions that they reach, and some principles that they establish, are, in the least, of doubtful validity.

2. Replacing the glorious thought and sound understanding of the early great pioneers and scholars of *Islām* (the *Salaf* (R)) by inferior opinions and speculations of later scholars.

These problems led to the following serious consequences:

- A deformation in some of the fundamental beliefs for the majority of *Muslims*, including many who are regarded as scholars.

- Practicing *Islām* in a way that does not conform with (and sometimes contradicts) the teachings of Muḥammad (S).

Through the ages, only few true scholars (*ʿulamāʾ*) have directed their efforts to correcting these problems through reviving the authentic *Sunnah* and fighting *bidʿah*s. Their efforts have always been greatly countered and fiercely rejected by their contemporaries. But there is no way to stop truth from spreading, and Allāh's Light will surely be complete and prevalent. These *ʿulamāʾ* (may Allāh bless them and reward their efforts) have produced marvelous writings which evaded the above mentioned pitfalls and rectified *Islām*ic beliefs and practices.

Very little of these great writings have been translated to English, or have been resorted to in English writings on *Islām*. Thus a good deal of the existing *Islām*ic literature in English suffers from the two problems cited earlier. It also suffers from additional problems, mainly:

3. Many writers have had a shallow *Islām*ic education. They had to self-educate themselves to meet the requirements of *daʿwah* in the West. But their education has not been, in general, adequate enough to qualify them to write on *Islām*.

4. Some non-*Muslim* scholars and orientalists have volunteered to write on *Islām*. Such persons' knowledge of *Islām* has been, in some instances, quite vast, both in breadth and depth. Yet,

---

1 *Ḥadīth*: Reports of the Prophet's sayings, actions, and approvals.

their writings are usually charged with obvious fallacies and prejudiced misinformation, whether intended or not.

These problems have caused a further deviation from the truth in many of today's English writings and talks on *Islām*.

This publication is, therefore, a humble response to our feeling of a great responsibility: the responsibility to help bring forth, before the general English speaking public, writings which refine *Islām*ic concepts from the above stated problems and which present *Islām* pure and simple, as close as possible to the way that it was understood and practiced by its early good pioneers - the *Salaf*.

Translating and Transliterating Arabic

Attempt has been made to minimize the use of Arabic terms. This is a frequently neglected service to the English speaking reader. Transliterated Arabic terms are used in the following two situations only:

a) When no English expression is found that can reflect the same meaning as the original term.

b) When it is judged that an Arabic term is of such importance that it is essential to familiarize the readers with it.

In such cases, Arabic terms are defined at their first occurrence, usually in footnotes. They are then include in the INDEX OF ARABIC TERMS appearing (if available) at the end of the book.

Except for proper nouns, transliterated Arabic terms are *italic*ized. In general, the rules of English pronunciation can be applied. The following table includes additional symbols employed in this book to help pronounce the Arabic terms.

Symbol	Stands for	English Equivalent Sounds
ā, Ā	*Alif* (long vowel a)	Mostly: Man, sad. At times: Father, hard, god.
ū, Ū	*Wāw* (long vowel u)	Root, soup, flute.
ī, Ī	*Yā'* (long vowel i)	Seed, lean, piece, receive.

Symbol	Stands for	English Equivalent Sounds
ʾ	*Hamzah*	The first consonant vocal sound uttered when saying: <u>a</u>t, <u>i</u>t or <u>o</u>h.
Th, th	*Thāʾ*	<u>Th</u>ree, mo<u>th</u>.
Ḥ, ḥ	*Ḥāʾ*	No equivalent. Produced in the lower throat, below "h". Resembles the sound produced after swallowing.
Kh, kh	*Khāʾ*	No equivalent. Produced in the back of the mouth and top of the throat.
<u>Th</u>, <u>th</u>	*<u>Th</u>āl*	<u>Th</u>ere, mo<u>th</u>er.
Ṣ, ṣ	*Ṣād*	A deeper "s" sound. Somewhat close to the "sc" in "mu<u>sc</u>le".
Ḍ, ḍ	*Ḍād*	Sounds fuller than a "d". Produced by touching the tongue to the mouth's roof.
Ṭ, ṭ	*Ṭah*	Sound fuller than a "t". Pro
Ẓ, ẓ	*Ẓah*	A deeper *<u>th</u>āl*, produced by touching the tip of the tongue to the back of the front teeth.
ʿ	*ʿAyn*	Produced in the bottom of the throat, underneath "ḥ".
Gh, gh	*Ghayn*	A gurgling sound produced in the back of the mouth, just above the *khāʾ*. Similar to the "R" in some french accents.
Q, q	*Qāf*	Somewhat similar to the "c" in "<u>c</u>offee".

Translating and Referencing *Qurʾān* and *Ḥadīth*

Special consideration has been taken in translating *Qurʾān*ic texts. The *Qurʾān* contains Allāh's exact words. These words cannot be exactly translated into other languages because of possible misinterpretations and limited human understanding. It is best to translate the meanings as understood by *Muslim* scholars. This is what is attempted here. When an *āyah* [1] is cited, the Arabic text is quoted first, followed, between double angle quotation marks («»), by the English meaning in **boldface**. The meaning is extracted from books of *tafsīr* (*Qurʾān*ic commentaries and interpretations) and from accessible translations.

The location of a *Qurʾān*ic citation is specified in a footnote. It provides the name of the *sūrah* (*Qurʾān*ic chapter) followed by its number and the number (or numbers) of the *āyāt* cited.

In general, the Arabic text of a cited *ḥadīth* is not provided. This is based on a general agreement among *ʿulamāʾ* permitting relating the *Ḥadīth* by meaning. The meaning of a *ḥadīth* is included, in **boldface**, between single angle quotation marks (‹›).

A footnote normally specifies the location of a cited *ḥadīth* in the *Ḥadīth* compilations. The footnote indicates as well its degree of authenticity and the names of scholars who made such judgement. If a *ḥadīth* is narrated by Al-Bukhārī or Muslim, its authenticity is taken for granted.

Mnemonics

Out of love, appreciation, gratitude or other related noble feelings, a *Muslim* is encouraged to utter certain phrases at the mention of Allāh, His messengers, the *ṣaḥābah* (Messenger's companions), or other righteous *Muslims*. For printing and space reasons, instead of presenting the complete phrases, the following mnemonics are employed where appropriate:

(T) Mnemonic of praising Allāh with phrases like "*Subḥānahū wa taʿālā*" ("He is above all weakness or indignity"), "*ʿAzza wa jall*" ("Supreme Power and Dignity belong to Him"), or "*Tabārak*" ("Exalted is He").

(S) Mnemonic of "*Ṣalla 'Llāhu ʿalayhi wa sallam*" ("May Allāh's peace and praise be on him"). This is uttered at the mention of

---

1 *Āyah*: In general, a *Qurʾān*ic sentence (sometimes longer or shorter than a full sentence).

Muḥammad or other messengers.

(R) Mnemonic of "*Raḍiya 'Llāhu ʿanhu*" ("May Allāh be pleased with him") or "*Raḍiya 'Llāhu ʿanhā*" ("May Allāh be pleased with her") or any plural thereof. This is uttered at the mention of one or more of the *ṣaḥābah*.

(r) Mnemonic of "*Raḥimahu 'Llāh*" ("May Allāh have mercy on him") or "*Raḥimaha 'Llāh*" ("May Allāh have mercy on her") or any plural thereof. This is uttered at the mention of past *ʿulamā'* and righteous *Muslim*s other than the *Ṣaḥābah*.

When coming across any of these mnemonics, the reader is advised to utter the complete phrase rather than the mnemonic letter which, in itself, has no useful value.

Acknowledgements

All praise and thanks be to Allāh for helping complete this work. In addition, deep appreciation and gratitude is expressed toward the large number of *Muslim*s who helped and supported this effort in various ways. It is very impractical to mention their names here, but their rewards surely rest with Allāh, *in shā'a 'Llāh*.

Appeal

Care has been taken here to present *Islām* in the most pure and accurate manner. Yet, no human work can be devoid of mistakes. We appeal to the readers who come across any mistakes in this work to ask Allāh to forgive us and to be kind enough, if possible, to write and point them out to us.

We ask Allāh (T) to make this humble effort helpful and fruitful, to forgive our shortcomings, to purify our work from hypocrisy and conceit, and to accept it from us.

Finally, we ask Allāh (T) to forgive all the believers and to bestow His peace and praise upon our Prophet Muḥammad.

The Publisher

PREFACE

The Author

BIRTH

The author of this book is Abū ʿAbdillāh, Shamsuddīn Muḥammad, son of Abū Bakr, son of Ayyūb, son of Saʿd, son of Ḥurayz, of Damascus. He is best known as Ibn ul-Qayyim (Son of the Custodian), named so after al-Jawziyyah school in Damascus which was under custody of his father. His family was one of honor and knowledge.

He was born on Ṣafar 7, 691 AH (1292 CE), in the village of Zarʿ, to the south-east of Damascus.

TEACHERS

He moved to Damascus and learned the *Islām*ic knowledge under a number of prominent scholars. His teachers included:

- His father;
- Ash-Shihāb un-Nābulsī;
- Judge Taqiyyuddīn bin Sulaymān;
- Abū Bakr bin ʿAbdiddāʾim;
- ʿĪssā al-Mutʿim;
- Ismāʿīl bin Maktūm;
- Fāṭimah bint Jawhar;
- Ṣafiyuddīn al-Hindī; and
- Ismāʿīl bin Muḥammad al-Ḥarrānī.

His most notable teacher was Aḥmad bin ʿAbdilḥalīm Ibn Taymiyyah. He valued him most and he stayed with him continuously in his years of youth: from 712 AH (1312 CE) until Ibn Taymiyyah's death in 728 AH (1328 CE). He loved him dearly, he comprehended his thought, and he worked on clarifying and spreading his knowledge and writings after his death.

THOUGHT AND METHODOLOGY

Going along the footsteps of his teacher Ibn Taymiyyah, Ibn ul-Qayyim was staunch in spreading the call to renovate *Islām* by adhering to the Book of Allāh (T) and the *Sunnah* of His Messenger (S), by learning and understanding them the way they were understood by the good early generations of *Muslims*, by rejecting all that conflicts with them, by cleansing the *Sunnah* from people's innovations during centuries of decline and ignorance, and by warning *Muslims* against all corruption that infiltrated into *Islām* through *Ṣūfī* fraud, Greek philosophy, and Indian renunciation.

WRITINGS

Ibn ul-Qayyim wrote more than sixty books in various areas of *Islām*. Some of these are:

- *ʿUddat uṣ-Ṣābirīna wa-Thakhīrat ush-Shākirīn;*
- *Al-Fawāʾid;*
- *Ar-Rūḥ;*
- *Aṣ-Ṣawāʿiq ul-Mursalatu ʿalal-Jahmiyyati wal-Muʿaṭṭilah*
- *Aṭ-Ṭuruq ul-Ḥukmiyyatu fis-Siyāsat ish-Sharʿiyyah;*
- *Badāʾiʿ ul-Fawāʾid;*
- *Ḥādil-Arwāḥi ilā Bilād il-Afrāḥ;*
- *Hidāyat ul-Ḥayārā fī Ajwibat il-Yahūdi wan-Naṣārā;*
- *Iʿlām ul-Muwaqqiʿīna ʿan Rabb il-ʿĀlamīn;*
- *Ijtimāʿ ul-Juyūsh il-Islāmiyyati ʿalā Ghazw il-Muʿaṭṭilati wal-Jahmiyyah;*
- *Ighāthat ul-Lahfāni min Makāʾid ish-Shayṭān;*
- *Madārij us-Sālikīna fī Manāzili Iyyaka Naʿbudu wa Iyyaka Nastaʿīn;*
- *Muftāḥu Dār is-Saʿādah;*
- *Rawḍat ul-Muḥibbīn;*
- *Shifāʾ ul-ʿAlīli fī Masāʾil il-Qaḍāʾi wal-Qadari wal-Ḥikmati wa 't-Taʿlīl;*
- *Ṭarīq ul-Hijratayni wa Bāb us-Saʿādatayn; and*
- *Zād ul-Maʿādi fī Hadyi Khayr il-ʿIbād.*

STUDENTS

Ibn ul-Qayyim had numerous students. Some of the more reputable among them are the following:

- Al-Ḥāfiẓ Abul-Faraj ʿAbdurraḥmān bin Aḥmad bin Rajab (died in 795 AH) - he stayed with him until his death in 751 AH;

- Al-Ḥāfiẓ Ismā'īl bin 'Umar bin Kathīr (died in 774 AH);
- Al-Ḥāfiẓ Muḥammad bin 'Abdilhādī (died in 744 AH);
- his two sons: Ibrāhīm and Sharafuddīn 'Abdullāh; and
- Shamsuddīn, Abū 'Abdillāh, Muḥammad bin 'Abdilqādir an-Nābulsī (died in 797 AH).

DEATH

He died on the evening of Thursday, Rajab 23, 751 AH (1350 CE). People prayed for him (the *Janāzah* prayer) on the following day in the Great Masjid in Damascus. He was buried in al-Bāb uṣ-Ṣaghīr cemetery.

He was highly praised by the *ulamā'* after him, such as al-Ḥāfiẓ Ibn Rajab, al-Ḥāfiẓ uth-Thahabī, Ibn Nāṣir id-Dimashqī, Judge Burhānuddīn az-Zar'ī, al-Ḥāfiẓ Ibn Ḥajar, and Muḥammad Ash-Shawkānī.

This Book

Despite its small size, this book is very important in explaining the True Methodology of adherence to Allāh's Book, His Messenger's *Sunnah*, and the Guidance of the *Ṣaḥābah*.

It starts by explaining the qualities of righteousness and piety, which the *Qur'ān* requires people to perform and enjoin. It evolves to describe the migration to Allāh (T) and His Messenger (S). Then it pictures the true misery and the true happiness of people. Toward the end, it recounts the requirements of the Journey of Migration, presenting along the way some very important insights for comprehending the *Qur'ān*.

In addition to its valuable methodological coverage, the book is very touching in its address to the soul and the heart. This is a characteristic that you rarely find in writings of other authors. May Allāh (T) reward Ibn ul-Qayyim profusely.

Abū 'Abdillāh Muḥammad al-Jibālī
Al-Muḥarram 1416 AH (May 1995 CE)

CHAPTER 1
RIGHTEOUSNESS AND PIETY

Introduction

The *shaykh*[1], *imām*[2], and *ʿallāmah*[3] Muḥammad bin Abī Bakr, better known as Ibnu Qayyim il-Jawziyyah, may Allāh be pleased with him and may He please him, said the following in his message from Tabūk[4] on the eighth of *al-Muḥarram*[5], 733 AH[6]: -

I glorify and praise Allāh with all the praise that He deserves. I ask Allāh to grant peace and distinguished honor to the Seal of His Prophets and Messengers, Muḥammad.

The Happiness of a Human Being

Allāh (T) says in His Book:

﴿وَتَعَاوَنُوا عَلَى ٱلْبِرِّ وَٱلتَّقْوَى، وَلَا تَعَاوَنُوا عَلَى ٱلْإِثْمِ وَٱلْعُدْوَانِ، وَٱتَّقُوا ٱللهَ، إِنَّ ٱللهَ شَدِيدُ ٱلْعِقَابِ﴾ المائدة ٢

1 *Shaykh*: Literally means and old man. It is commonly used as a title of respect for a man of better *Islām*ic knowledge. It is also used in some Arab countries as a title of authority similar to "prince".

2 *Imām*: *Islām*ic leader. It usually refers to one who leads the prayers, to one with a superior knowledge of *Islām*, or to a ruler.

3 *ʿAllāmah*: A great scholar. This is an exaggerated form of *ʿālim* (pl. *ʿulamāʾ*) meaning scholar.

4 Tabūk is a village on the northern territory of the Arab Peninsula, close to the border of Palestine.

5 *Al-Muḥarram*: The first month of the *Islām*ic lunar calendar.

6 AH: Abbreviation for "After *Hijrah*". The *Islām*ic (*Hijrī*) calendar starts on the year that Prophet Muḥammad (S) migrated from Makkah to al-Madīnah. This corresponds to 622 CE (Christian Era). Being lunar, the *Hijrī* year is 11 days shorter than the solar year, which makes a difference of one year every 33 years. Thus, to convert AH years to CE years you need to do the following:

$$CE = 622 + AH - (AH \div 33).$$

From this, we can obtain the reciprocal conversion as follows:

$$AH = (CE - 622) \times (33 \div 32).$$

We deduce that this book was written on 1333 CE.

«... Help one another in *birr*[1] and *taqwā*[2], and do not help one another in sinning and transgression. And fear and revere Allāh; verily, Allāh is severe in punishment.» [3]

This *āyah* [4] comprises all that is good for people in this life and in the hereafter, both among themselves and between themselves and their Lord (Allāh). This is so because man will always be dealing with one of two situations or obligations. The first is that between him and Allāh (T), and the other is that between him and other people.

The duty of a person toward his fellow human beings is that his company with them should be directed toward helping one another to please and obey Allāh. This is the ultimate happiness and success of a human being. One can have no happiness otherwise. This is the "*birr* and *taqwā*", which encompass the whole *Dīn* [5].

It should be pointed out that when either "*birr*" or "*taqwā*" is mentioned, the other word is implied, or follows in a logical sense. The reason for this is that "righteousness" carries the meaning of "piety" and vice versa. But when they appear together, as they do here, each word takes a distinctive meaning. Similar to this are the pairs of terms:

Īmān[6] versus *Islām*,
Īmān versus good deeds,
faqīr (a poor man) versus *miskīn* (a needy man),
fusūq (rebellion against Allāh) versus *ʿisyān* (disobedience),
munkar (rejected deeds in *Islām*) versus *fāḥishah* (great sinning),

and so on. Comprehending this important rule helps eliminate some misconceptions that people have [7].

1 *Birr*: Righteousness, virtue, goodness and related meanings.
2 *Taqwā*: Piety, fear, reverence, and related meanings presented before Allāh.
3 *Al-Māʾidah* 5:2.
4 *Āyah*: Literally means a miracle and a sign. The *Qurʾān* is a miracle in itself, and so is any portion of it. The smallest subdivision of the *Qurʾān*ic text is thus called an *āyah*. An *āyah* is usually one sentence in length, but is sometimes more than one sentence, and sometimes only a part of a sentence. The plural of *āyah* is *āyāt*.
5 *Dīn*: The Religion (of *Islām*) with all its beliefs and practices.
6 *Īmān*: The required beliefs in *Islām*. The texts of the *Qurʾān* and the *Sunnah* reveal that *Īmān* includes good deeds, and that it increases and decreases depending on the deeds.
7 This will be discussed further in the next few pages.

Birr in Relation to *Taqwā*

Birr is the excellence, virtue and goodness present in something. This follows from the root and the derivation of this word in Arabic. Related to it is *burr* (wheat), which surpasses other grains in benefits and goodness. Also, a good man is described as *bārr* (fulfilling his promises) or *barr* (merciful and kind). Allāh described the angels as *bararah* (pious and just) and the paradise dwellers as *abrār* (righteous).

Birr then comprises all kinds of goodness and perfection expected in a human being. Opposite to it is *ithm*[1]. An-Nuwās bin Sim'ān (R) reported that the Prophet (S) said:

> **‹*Birr* is good manners, and *ithm* is those [evil] thoughts that weave about in your chest and you fear that other people may know about them.›** [2,3]

Under the meaning of *birr* comes *Īmān* with all its apparent and concealed manifestations; and *taqwā* is certainly included in this meaning.

Birr is frequently used to describe the heart, and to indicate whether it possesses the true taste and sweetness of *Īmān*. It implies feelings of serenity, satisfaction, strength and pleasure that enter the heart because of *Īmān*. Indeed, *Īmān* produces happiness, sweetness and delight in the heart. One who does not experience this lacks or misses *Īmān*, and is among those described by Allāh (T) as:

﴿قَالَتِ ٱلْأَعْرَابُ آمَنَّا، قُل لَّمْ تُؤْمِنُوا، وَلَـٰكِن قُولُوا أَسْلَمْنَا، وَلَمَّا يَدْخُلِ ٱلْإِيمَانُ فِي قُلُوبِكُمْ﴾ الحجرات ١٤

> **«The Bedouins say, "We believe." Say [Muḥammad]: "You believe not, but you can only say, 'We have submitted to you as *Muslims*,' for *Īmān* has not yet entered your hearts ..."»** [4]

---

1 *Ithm*: Sinning.

2 Recorded by Muslim and others.

3 Also, Wābiṣah bin Ma'bid (R) reported that the Messenger of Allāh (S) said to him:

> **‹You want to know about *birr* and *ithm*? O Wābiṣah, check your heart! *Birr* is that which pacifies the soul and comforts the heart, and *ithm* is that which weaves [evil thoughts] in the heart and echoes in the chest, despite what other people advise you.›**

This is recorded by Aḥmad, and judged authentic by al-Munthirī and others.

4 *Al-Ḥujurāt* 49:14.

The *'ulamā'* have two views regarding these Bedouins. The more appropriate view is that they were *Muslim*s, not hypocrites. Yet they were not full believers because *Īmān* had not yet entered and truly touched their hearts.

Allāh (T) includes the various qualities of *birr* in the following *āyah*:

﴿لَيْسَ ٱلْبِرَّ أَن تُوَلُّوا وُجُوهَكُمْ قِبَلَ ٱلْمَشْرِقِ وَٱلْمَغْرِبِ، وَلَـٰكِنَّ ٱلْبِرَّ مَنْ آمَنَ بِٱللَّهِ وَٱلْيَوْمِ ٱلْآخِرِ وَٱلْمَلَائِكَةِ وَٱلْكِتَابِ وَٱلنَّبِيِّينَ، وَآتَى ٱلْمَالَ عَلَى حُبِّهِ ذَوِي ٱلْقُرْبَى وَٱلْيَتَامَى وَٱلْمَسَاكِينَ وَٱبْنَ ٱلسَّبِيلِ وَٱلسَّائِلِينَ وَفِي ٱلرِّقَابِ، وَأَقَامَ ٱلصَّلَاةَ وَآتَى ٱلزَّكَاةَ، وَٱلْمُوفُونَ بِعَهْدِهِمْ إِذَا عَاهَدُوا، وَٱلصَّابِرِينَ فِي ٱلْبَأْسَاءِ وَٱلضَّرَّاءِ وَحِينَ ٱلْبَأْسِ، أُوْلَـٰئِكَ ٱلَّذِينَ صَدَقُوا، وَأُوْلَـٰئِكَ هُمُ ٱلْمُتَّقُونَ﴾ البقرة ١٧٧

> «It is not righteousness that you turn your faces toward the East or the West [in prayers], but righteousness is he who believes in Allāh, the Last Day, the Angels, the Book, and the Prophets, and he who gives his wealth, in spite of the love for it, to kinfolk, to orphans, to the needy, to the wayfarer, to those who ask, and he who sets slaves free, and he who establishes prayers, and gives the purifying charity, and those who fulfill their covenant when they make it, and those who are patient in extreme poverty and ailment, and at the time of fighting during the battle, such are the people of truth, and they are the pious.»[1]

Allāh informs here that believing in Him, in His angels, in His Messengers and in the Last Day are all required acts of *birr*. These are the five articles of faith without which *Īmān* cannot survive.

He (T) then mentions that the apparent acts of performing *ṣalāh*[2] and giving *zakāh*[3] and other forms of mandatory expenditures are also acts of *birr*.

Then He mentions that *birr* also comprises concealed deeds of the heart, such as steadfastness and fulfilling the covenants.

The deeds mentioned in this *āyah* thus cover all aspects of the *Dīn*: the essentials and the rituals - deeds of the heart and of the body, as

---

1   *Al-Baqarah* 2:177.
2   *Ṣalāh*: The *Islām*ic prescribed prayers.
3   *Zakāh*: Mandatory prescribed alms.

well as the five pillars of *Īmān*. At the end of the *āyah*, Allāh (T) tells that these are also qualities of *taqwā* [1].

Taqwā in Relation to *Birr*

Taqwā is to abide by Allāh's commands and prohibitions with *Īmān* and *iḥtisāb* [2]. Thus one would obey Allāh's commands, believing in them and in the rewards He promised for them, and would also avoid His prohibitions, believing in them and fearing His retribution for those who commit them.

This is similar to what Ṭalq bin Ḥabīb [3] said, "If ordeal appears amongst you extinguish it with *taqwā*." When asked, "What is *taqwā*?" He replied:

> "It is to act in obedience to Allāh, with light (guidance) from Allāh, seeking Allāh's reward, and to avoid disobeying Allāh, with light from Allāh, fearing His punishment." [4]

This is one of the best definitions of *taqwā*. Every deed requires an origin and a destination. A deed would not count as an act of obedience, and would not bring a person closer to Allāh, unless it originates from sincere *Īmān*. This then, and not habits, desires, showoff and so forth, should be what initiates such an act. The destination should be to attain Allāh's rewards and acceptance. This is the meaning of *iḥtisāb*.

These two essential requirements for a good deed, i.e. *Īmān* and *iḥtisāb*, occur together frequently in *Ḥadīth* [5]. For instance, the Messenger (S) said:

> **‹Whoever fasts *Ramaḍān* with *Īmān* and *iḥtisāb* will have his previous sins forgiven.›**

And he said:

---

1 The pious or *muttaqūn*: those who possess *taqwā*.

2 *Iḥtisāb*: To count on Allāh's promised rewards for a given deed.

3 Ṭalq bin Ḥabīb al-ʿAnazī is one of the famous *Tābiʿīn*.. He was known for his knowledge and piety, and his voice was beautiful in reading the *Qur'ān*.

4 These words of Ṭalq were recorded by Ibn ul-Mubārak in *az-Zuhd* and Abū Nuʿaym in *al-Ḥulyah*. They were authenticated by al-Albānī in *al-Īmān* of Ibn Abī Shaybah.

5 *Ḥadīth*: Literally means talk. It usually refers to what was reported of the Prophet's words, actions or tacit approvals. In this sense, it is a synonym to the *Sunnah*.

‹Whoever stands up [in prayer] on the Night of *Qadr*[1] with *Īmān* and *iḥtisāb* will have his previous sins forgiven.› [2]

What Ṭalq said, "... with light from Allāh ..." points to the first requirement, *Īmān*, that should be the origin of a deed and the reason for initiating it. His words, "... seeking Allāh's reward ..." point to the second requirement, *iḥtisāb*, which is the purpose and goal of a deed.

Thus *taqwā*, without doubt, comprises all the fundamental and complementary elements of *Īmān*. It, therefore, comprises the meaning of *birr* as well.

"*Birr* and *Taqwā*" and Other Pairs of Words

When these two words *birr* and *taqwā* appear together, as in **«Help one another in *birr* and *taqwā* ...»** above, then there is a difference in their meaning. This is similar to the difference between a means and a purpose.

Birr is sought for its own; it represents the integrity and excellence of a human being; one cannot attain any virtue without it, as was discussed earlier.

Taqwā, on the other hand, is the means and way leading to *birr*. The root of the word in Arabic means "protection". One practicing it protects himself from the Fire. Protection is not sought for itself as much as to prevent harm. Thus the relationship of *birr* and *taqwā* is similar to that of health (which is a purpose) and care for the body (which is a means).

Knowing such difference in the meanings of related pairs of words, when separated or combined, is important. It is very valuable in understanding some expressions and implications in the *Qur'ān*, and in knowing the ordinances that Allāh (T) revealed to His Messenger (S). Allāh (T) blames in His Book those who ignore His ordinances [3].

Lacking this knowledge leads to two great dangers:

1) The first is that one would include under a given term an unintended meaning, treating equally matters which Allāh

---

1 *Qadr*: Honor and Distinction. The most blessed night of the year is the Night of *Qadr*. It is one of the nights of the month of *Ramaḍān*. On it, Allāh's mercy descends abundantly. The *Qur'ān* was first revealed on one such night.

2 This and the previous *ḥadīth* were narrated by Abū Hurayrah (R) and recorded by al-Bukhārī and Muslim.

3 Refer to *at-Tawbah* 9:27.

made distinct.

2) The other danger is that one would exclude from a term some meanings to which it should apply, changing by that the ordinances and separating matters which Allāh had combined.

A sage person comprehends this and other similar rules and understands that many deviations have been caused by ignoring this. Detailing this matter cannot be covered even in a large volume.

An example of this is *khamr*[1]. It is a general term referring to all intoxicants; one may not exclude some intoxicants and remove the ordinance of prohibition from them.

The same argument applies to the prohibition of various forms of *maysir* (gambling). It applies to *nikāḥ* (lawful marriage); one may not including in its meaning some unlawful forms of marriage. It applies to *ribā*[2]; one may not exclude from the prohibition any usury-based dealings, or include dealings which are not usury-based. It applies also to other term such as transgression and justice, good and evil, and so on.

Sinning and Transgression

Therefore, what is required from people in their gathering and company is to help one another in *birr* and *taqwā*. Each one should help his companion with knowledge and action. One person cannot do this by himself. Allāh's wisdom has decreed that the existence of human beings should be through mutual help and support.

In the above *āyah* (*al-Mā'idah* 2), **«... but do not help one another in *ithm* (sin) and *'udwān* (transgression) ...»**. Forbidding *ithm* and *'udwān* is parallel to enjoining *birr* and *taqwā*. The difference between *ithm* and *'udwān* is that *ithm* applies to deeds which are prohibited in themselves (ex. adultery, drinking liquor, stealing.) *'Udwān*, on the other hand, applies to deeds that exceed the limits set by Allāh (T) (ex. marrying a fifth wife or demanding more than one's right in blood ransom.) Allāh (T) said:

﴿تِلْكَ حُدُودُ ٱللهِ فَلَا تَعْتَدُوهَا، وَمَنْ يَتَعَدَّ حُدُودَ ٱللهِ فَأُوْلَٰئِكَ هُمُ ٱلظَّٰلِمُونَ﴾ البقرة ٢٢٩

1 *Khamr*: Alcoholic liquors.

2 *Ribā*: Usury. It includes many form of dealings in which money produces money without toil or risk.

«... These are the limits ordained by Allāh, so do not transgress them. Whoever transgresses the limits ordained by Allāh, then such are the wrong doers.» [1]

And He said:

﴿تِلْكَ حُدُودُ ٱللهِ فَلَا تَقْرَبُوهَا﴾ البقرة ١٨٧

«... These are the limits set by Allāh, so do not approach them.» [2]

He (T) forbids transgressing His limits in the first *āyah,* and approaching them in the second. Allāh's limits separate between *ḥalāl* [3] and *ḥarām* [4]. In some cases they are part of the prohibition, and thus may not be transgressed. In other cases they are not included in the prohibition, and one is instructed to stay away from them [as a safety measure].

The Two Obligations

In association with people, one has the obligation to help them, with both his knowledge and actions, to act according to *birr* and *taqwā*.

And one's obligation toward his Lord (T) is to favor observing His commands and avoid disobedience. He should fear and revere Him as was mentioned earlier (*al-Mā'idah* 2).

Thus there are two obligations on every human being: one toward the creation and the other toward the Creator.

One cannot fulfill the first obligation unless he detaches himself from the evils of people, sincerely offering them advice, being good to them, and caring about their well-being.

And one cannot fulfill the other obligation unless he eliminates all creatures from between himself and Allāh (T), and does so with sincerity, love and adoration.

One should comprehend this subtle matter, because any fault in fulfilling either of these two obligations is caused by a negligence either in knowledge or in practice.

This is the meaning of what Shaykh ʿAbdul-Qādir al-Jīlānī, may

1 *Al-Baqarah* 2:229.

2 *Al-Baqarah* 2:187.

3 *Ḥalāl*: Things that are permissible in the *Islām*ic law.

4 *Ḥarām*: Things that are prohibited in the *Islām*ic law.

Allāh bless his soul, said:

> "Let not [your attachment to] the people come between you and *al-Ḥaqq* [1], and let not [favoring] yourself come between you and the people. If one does not do this, he will be in continued confusion, and his affairs will always be at loss."

1 *Al-Ḥaqq*: the Truth. This is one of Allāh's names.

CHAPTER 2
MIGRATION TO ALLĀH

Migration of the Heart

The caravan departs, and the traveller enters into a foreign land. He becomes separated from the habits and customs associated with his homeland. This allows him to ponder carefully over his situation. He seeks the most important thing that helps in his journey to Allāh, and that deserves his life's pursuance.

The One in whose Hand is the guidance guides him to this most important thing that he seeks: "Migration to Allāh and His Messenger". This migration is a *farḍ*[1] on everyone at all times - it is the thing that Allāh (T) requires from his *'ibād*[2].

Migration is of two types:

1) The first is the migration of the body from one land to another. The legislation regarding this type of migration is well known, and it is not our intention to discuss them here.

2) The second type is the migration of the heart to Allāh (T) and His Messenger (S). This is the only true *hijrah*; it must precede the bodily *hijrah*, which is its natural outcome.

Fleeing unto Allāh

This *hijrah* requires an origin and a goal. A person migrates with his heart:

from	loving other than Allāh	to	loving Him;
from	fearing and hoping and relying on other than Him	to	fearing and hoping and relying on Him;

1 *Farḍ*: Mandatory *Islāmic* duty.

2 *'Ibād*: This (or *'abīd*) is a plural of *'abd*, which means slave or servant. In reference to Allāh (T), it usually means a devout worshiper (as in *'Abd Ullāh*). But it frequently refers to a "human being" because every human being is subdued by Allāh (T) whether one admits it or not.

from	calling upon, asking, surrendering to, and humbling oneself before other than Him	to calling upon, asking, surrendering to, and humbling oneself before Him.

This is precisely the meaning of "fleeing unto Allāh", as He (T) says:

﴿فَفِرُّوا إِلَى ٱللَّهِ﴾ الذاريات ٥٠

«...Flee unto Allāh...» [1]

And indeed, the *tawḥīd* [2] required from a person is to flee from Allāh unto Him! Under this heading of "from" and "to" falls a great reality of *tawḥīd*.

Fleeing unto Allāh (T) includes turning to Him only for asking or worship or anything which proceeds from that. Thus, it includes the *tawḥīd* of *Ilāhiyyah* which was the common point in the messages of all the messengers, may Allāh's bestow His praise and peace upon all of them.

On the other hand, fleeing from Allāh (unto Him) includes the *tawḥīd* of *Rubūbiyyah* and the belief in the *Qadar* [3]. It is the belief that whatever one hates or fears or flees from in the universe takes place by the Will of Allāh alone. What He (T) wills will surely happen, and what He does not will never be and is impossible to happen.

Thus when a person flees unto Allāh, he would be fleeing unto him from a thing that occurred by His Will. In other words, he would be fleeing from Him unto Him!

---

1 *Ath-Thāriyāt* 51:50.

2 *Tawḥīd*: Accepting and believing in the oneness. In reference to Allāh (T), it means to believe in:

(a) His existence and ownership of the creation, which is sometimes referred to as the *Tawḥīd* of *Rubūbiyyah* (state of being the only True Lord or *Rabb*).

(b) His possession of the highest attributes and most excellent names, which is sometimes referred to as the *Tawḥīd* of Names and Attributes.

(c) Him as being solely worthy of worship and full obedience, which is sometimes referred to as the *Tawḥīd* of *'Ubūdiyyah* or *'Ibādah* (worship), or of *Ilāhiyyah* or *Ulūhiyyah* (state of being the only True God or *Ilāh*).

In reference to the Messenger (S), it is to believe in the uniqueness of his Message and in the obligation to follow him exclusively. This is sometimes referred to as the *Tawḥīd* of *Ittibā'* (adherence).

3 *Qadar*: Allāh's Divine Measure and Decree.

One who understands this well can then understand the meaning of the Messenger's (S) words:

> **‹… I seek refuge from You in You …›** [1]

And:

> **‹… There is no shelter or escape from You except in You …›** [2]

There is nothing in the universe that one would flee or seek protection from but is created and originated by Allāh (T). Hence, one would flee from that which emanates from Allāh's decree, will, and creation, to that which emanates from His mercy, goodness, kindness, and bounty. One is, therefore, fleeing from Allāh unto Him, and seeking refuge in Him from Him!

Understanding these two matters causes one's heart to stop being attached to other than Allāh in fear, hope or love. He would then know that all that he flees from exists by the Allāh's will, power and creation. This would not leave in his heart any fear of other than his Creator and Maker. This in turn causes him to turn to Allāh alone in fear, love and hope.

Had it been that what one flees from were not under Allāh's Will and Power, one would then be excused to fear that thing instead of Allāh. This would be like running away from a creature to a more powerful one, without being totally confident that the second creature

---

1 This is a part from a *ḥadīth* recorded by Muslim and narrated by 'Ā'ishah (R) who said, "I missed Allāh's Messenger (S) one night. Then [after some search] my hand hit the soles of his feet in the *Masjid*. He had them erected (in *sujūd* (prostration)) and was saying:

> **‹O Allāh! I seek refuge from Your wrath in Your acceptance, from Your punishment in Your pardon, and from You in You!›**"

2 This is a part of a *ḥadīth* recorded by al-Bukhārī and Muslim and narrated by al-Barā' bin 'Āzib who said that the Messenger (S) instructed a man to say when he goes to bed:

> **‹O Allāh! I submit myself to You, and turn my face unto You, and support my back unto You, and rely in my affairs on You, hoping in You and fearing You; there is no shelter or escape from You except in You! I believe in the Book that You have revealed and in the Messenger that You have sent.›**

Then he (S) said, **‹Whoever says this and dies, he would die according to the *fiṭrah* (pure nature).›**

is powerful enough to protect him from the first one.

This is quite different from the case of a person who knows that the One to whom he is running is the same as the One who decreed, willed, and created that from which he is fleeing. In the latter case, no interest in seeking other protectors should remain in the heart.

So, understand well this important meaning in the Prophet's (S) words above. People have explained them in many different ways, yet very few have realized this meaning which is their core and moral. This facilitation [in understanding] is indeed from Allāh.

Thus the whole matter resolves to fleeing from Allāh unto Him. This is the meaning of the *hijrah* to Allāh (T). This further explains why the Messenger (S) said:

> **‹A true migrator is one who abandons what Allāh has prohibited.›** [1]

This is also why Allāh (T) mentions *Īmān* and *hijrah* together in several places [2] - the two being closely linked, and each of them requiring the other.

The Importance of Migrating to Allāh

In conclusion, the *hijrah* to Allāh includes abandoning what He hates and doing what He loves and accepts. The *hijrah* originates from feelings of love and hatred. The migrator from one place to another must have more love for the place to which he migrated than that from which he migrated, and these feelings are what led him to prefer one of the two places.

One's *nafs* [3], his whims and his devil keep calling him to that which is against what he loves and is satisfied with. One continues to be tested by these three things, calling him to avenues that displease his Lord.

At the same time, the call of *Īmān* will continue to direct him to what pleases his Lord. Thus one should keep migrating to Allāh at all times, and should not abandon this *hijrah* until death.

---

1 This is a part of a *ḥadīth* recorded by al-Bukhārī and narrated by ʿAbdullāh bin ʿAmr (R) that the Prophet (S) said:

> **‹A *Muslim* is one whom other *Muslims* are safe of his tongue and hand; and a migrator is one who deserts what Allāh has prohibited.›**

2 See, for example, *al-Anfāl* 8:72,74,75 and *at-Tawbah* 9:20.

3 *Nafs*: Self, soul or spirit. In the present context it refers to the lustful self which entices a person to do bad deeds.

This *hijrah* becomes strong or weak [in the heart] depending on the state of the *Īmān*. The stronger and more complete that the *Īmān* is, the more perfect the *hijrah*. And if the *Īmān* weakens, the *hijrah* weakens too, until one becomes unable to detect its presence or have the readiness to be moved by it.

What is surprising is that you might find a man talking at great length and going into very fine details regarding the [physical] *hijrah* from the land of disbelief (*Dār ul-Kufr*) to the land of *Islām* (*Dār ul-Islām*), and regarding the *hijrah* which ended with conquering Makkah, even though this type of *hijrah* is incidental, and he may never have to do a thing with it in his whole life. [1]

But as for the *hijrah* of the heart, which continues to be required from him as long as he breathes, you find that he does not seek any knowledge regarding it, nor does he develop any intention to undertake it! Thus he turns away from that for which he has been created, and which - alone - can save him, and involves himself in that which, of itself, cannot save him. This is the situation of those whose vision has been blinded, and whose knowledge is weak regarding the priorities of knowledge and action.

Indeed, Allāh is the One from Whom we seek help, and He alone does facilitate our matters. There is no god except Him and no Lord other than Him.

---

1 This applies mostly to a person who is already in a land of *Islām*, and who does not need to undertake this kind of physical *hijrah*.

CHAPTER 3

MIGRATION TO THE MESSENGER

Description of a Migrator to the Messenger

Migration to the Messenger (S) is a knowledge that has been [mostly] lost [from among people]; only its name continues to exist. It is a practice that has been abandoned; only its outline remains. It is a road whose milestones have been obliterated by wild animals, and whose water sources have been dried up by the enemies.

Thus the person who takes this road is a stranger among people, unique in his surroundings, distant [from others] despite his physical closeness, lonely despite numerous neighbors. He is unhappy with what pleases [the common] people, and [often] satisfied with what depresses them. He resides when they travel, and travels when they reside. He is alone in the Way that he chose for seeking his goal, feeling no satisfaction until he achieves it. He is with the people in his body, but away from them by virtue of his goal. Their eyes sleep indifferently, neglecting to seek the Guidance; but he spends his nights awake. They are too lazy for migration to the Prophet (S), while he is totally engrossed in its pursuit. They scorn his indifference to their ideas; and they blame him for criticizing their ignorance and inconsistencies. They cast their doubts on him, and they keep close watch over him.

They wait hopefully for death to rid them of him. He responds to them with what Allāh says:

﴿قُلْ هَلْ تَرَبَّصُونَ بِنَا إِلَّا إِحْدَى ٱلْحُسْنَيَيْنِ، وَنَحْنُ نَتَرَبَّصُ بِكُمْ أَنْ يُصِيبَكُمُ ٱللَّهُ بِعَذَابٍ مِنْ عِنْدِهِ أَوْ بِأَيْدِينَا، فَتَرَبَّصُوا إِنَّا مَعَكُمْ مُتَرَبِّصُونَ﴾ التوبة ٥٢

«Say [Muḥammad]: "Do you await for us anything except one of the two best things (martyrdom or victory), while we await for you that Allāh will afflict you with a punishment from Himself or at our hands. So wait, we too are waiting with you."» [1]

And: ﴿قَالَ رَبِّ ٱحْكُمْ بِٱلْحَقِّ، وَرَبُّنَا ٱلرَّحْمَٰنُ ٱلْمُسْتَعَانُ عَلَىٰ مَا تَصِفُونَ﴾ الأنبياء ٢١١

1 *At-Tawbah* 9:52.

«He (Muḥammad) said: "My Lord! Judge You in truth! Our Lord is ar-Raḥmān (the Most Merciful), whose help is to be sought against that which you attribute unto Him [of falsehoods]."»[1]

He further reminds them [with what an Arab poet once said]:

"Both we and you will die,
And the true loser at the time of reckoning is he who will then feel sorry."

Definition of Migration to the Messenger

Migration to the Prophet (S) is a most important matter. It is a long and difficult way for those who are not prepared for it, as a poet once said:

"It is far for him who is lazy or who tires easily,
But as for the one who has the longing, it is smooth and easy for him."

By Allāh's Life, this migration is but a shining light to illuminate your darkness. It is a full moon lighting the earth from east to west and capable of lighting your gloom. It is a clear sweet stream of water capable of washing away the stains of your heart. It is the beginning of a great bounty of which you could be unaware.

Listen now to the importance of this migration and to the evidence pointing to it. Be a judge of yourself before Allāh: Are you among those who run away from it or among those who run toward it?

The definition of this migration is: **the soul's journey, in all matters of belief, in all desires of the heart, and in all legislative matters, to the origin of Guidance and the source of Light.** This Guidance and Light came from the mouth of the truthful and trustworthy, Muḥammad (S), whom Allāh (T) describes as:

﴿مَا ضَلَّ صَاحِبُكُمْ وَمَا غَوَى، وَمَا يَنْطِقُ عَنِ ٱلْهَوَى، إِنْ هُوَ إِلَّا وَحْيٌ يُوحَى﴾ النجم ٢-٤

«Your companion (Muḥammad) is neither astray nor being misled. Nor does he speak of (his own)

1 *Al-Anbiyā'* 21:112.

desire. It is only the Revelation with which he is inspired.»[1]

A matter is acceptable only if the light of his Message shone over it; otherwise, it deserves to be thrown into the seas of darkness. A witness is acceptable only if he is recommended by this praised one (S); otherwise, you can consider him among the doubtful and accused.

How then could a man who is enslaved by his base instincts and worldly habits undertake this migration? A man who does not want to part with the place where he was born and raised? A man who says: "We only follow our fathers' ways, hold to their traditions, and trace their footsteps." How could he undertake it when his ancestors were incapable of doing so, and yet he relies totally on them to determine his way for success and salvation, claiming that their opinions should be better and sounder than his?

If you investigate the reason for saying this you find it a combination of laziness and indifference.

The Obligation of Migrating to the Messenger

This migration [to the Messenger (S)] is required from every *Muslim*. It follows directly from the [second part of the] *Shahādah* [2]:

> "Muḥammad (S) is Allāh's Messenger,"

just as the first type of migration [to Allāh] follows from the [first part of the same] *Shahādah*, that:

> "There is no true god except Allāh."

Every human being will be asked about these two manners of migration, both in the *barzakh* [3] and on the Day of Resurrection. Qatādah [one of the *Tābiʿīn*[4]] said:

> "The earlier and the later people will be asked two questions [on the Day of Judgement]: What did you

1 *An-Najm* 53:2-4.

2 *Shahādah*: The testimony proclaimed by every *Muslim*: that there is no true god except Allāh, and that Muḥammad (S) is Allāh's Messenger.

3 *Barzakh*: The period of death between the first life and the Resurrection.

4 *Tābiʿūn* or *tābiʿīn*: Plural of *tābiʿ* or *tābiʿiyy* (follower), which normally refers to a disciple of the *Ṣaḥābah* (Companions of the Messenger (S)).

worship, and what was your response to the messengers."[1]

These two matters are the content of the two parts of the *Shahādah*.

A Great Oath

Allāh (T) said:

﴿فَلَا وَرَبِّكَ لَا يُؤْمِنُونَ حَتَّىٰ يُحَكِّمُوكَ فِيمَا شَجَرَ بَيْنَهُمْ ثُمَّ لَا يَجِدُوا فِي أَنفُسِهِمْ حَرَجًا مِّمَّا قَضَيْتَ وَيُسَلِّمُوا تَسْلِيمًا﴾ النساء ٦٥

«But no, by your Lord, they can have no *Īmān* until they set you (Muḥammad) judge in any disputes that arise among them, and then find in their souls no resistance against your decisions but accept them with the fullest submission.»[2]

Here Allāh the Exalted makes the greatest oath - by His own Self, Glory be to Him, that the *Īmān* is not confirmed for a person, and he is not one of its People, until he accepts the Messenger (S) as the judge in all matters of dispute and in all aspects of the *Dīn*.

Using the term "any disputes" in this *āyah* absolutely negates the presence of *Īmān* unless the Messenger (S) is made the judge in all disputes. In addition, Allāh (T) has required satisfaction of the heart with the Messenger's judgment so that one would find no resistance in his soul. One should accept his judgment with satisfaction and submission. Taking the judgment with dissatisfaction, or following it in spite of oneself is contrary to the meaning of *Īmān*. So, the Messenger's judgment should be accepted with satisfaction and pleasure of the heart.

Once a person knows this, he should always examine himself and look into his heart [to see how true is his submission to the Messenger's judgements]. He should do this whenever a judgment comes from the Messenger (S), in a major or a minor matter, conflicting with his desire or differing from the way of his ancestors. Allāh (T) says:

﴿بَلِ ٱلْإِنسَانُ عَلَىٰ نَفْسِهِ بَصِيرَةٌ. وَلَوْ أَلْقَىٰ مَعَاذِيرَهُ﴾ القيامة ١٤-١٥

---

1 Ibn ul-Qayyim also attributed these words to Qatādah in *Ighāthat ul-Lahfān*. But he attributed them in *Madārij us-Sālikīn* to Abul ʿĀliyah. Ibn Jarīr aṭ-Ṭabarī also attributed them to Abul ʿĀliyah, as is mentioned by Ibn Kathīr in his *Tafsīr*. This derives from what Allāh (T) said in His Book (review *al-Qaṣaṣ* 28:62-74).

2 *An-Nisā'* 4:65.

«Nay, man will be evidence against himself, even though he were to put up excuses.» [1]

Glory be to Allāh! In how many instances have people hated quotations [from the Messenger (S)] and wished that they were never said! What hatred in their hearts and what dryness in their throats did some of the texts leave! Their secret thoughts will be revealed to them, causing them pain and humiliation on that Day:

﴿يَوْمَ تُبْلَى ٱلسَّرَائِرُ﴾ الطارق ٩

«The Day when all the secrets [of hearts and intentions] will be uncovered and tested.» [2]

Furthermore, Allāh (T) concludes the above *āyah* by requiring the fullest submission to [the judgements and commands of] the Messenger (S).

Loving the Messenger and Submitting to Him

This submission is not that of a defeated fighter who is forced to surrender to his enemy.

Rather, it is the submission of an obedient subordinate to his master who is dearer to him than any other creature, when he realizes that only through this submission will he achieve happiness and success.

It is the submission of one who realizes that, compared to his own self, this master has more concern and compassion for him, and is a better counselor who is more knowledgeable about what benefits him, and therefore more capable of saving him.

When a person realizes these meanings [3] with respect to the

---

1 *Al-Qiyāmah* 75:14-15.

2 *Aṭ-Ṭāriq* 86:9.

3 When applied to the Prophet (S), these meanings must be understood within the boundaries of *Islām*. They should not be influenced by extreme tendencies like the *ṣūfis*' who glorify him beyond his honorable human status, bestowing on him some divine attributes, and believing that he can answer the supplications and help and protect people while he is in his grave.

Thus he (S) should be (next to Allāh) dearer to a person than his own self; to submit to him means to submit to his *Sunnah*; his mercy and compassion and ability to counsel and save the people are by virtue of what Allāh (T) has taught him, and, after his death, this takes place through his *Sunnah* and teachings.

Messenger (S), he will surely submit himself to him (S), and surrender every desire in his heart in obedience to him. He will then comprehend that he cannot attain happiness except through this submission and obedience.

This matter is not easy to express in words. The heart needs to open up for it to allow it to sink down to its depths. It cannot be attained by mere claims or wishes. A poet once said:

> "Everyone claims to be the lover of Laylā,
> But Laylā does not commit to any of them."

There is a great difference between knowing the meaning of love and being truly in love. People frequently confuse between knowledge and experience.

Similar to this is the example of a sick man who is under the influence of a disease; he knows the meaning of health and well-being; however, his knowledge does not make him experience what a healthy man enjoys of good health, even if the latter cannot describe his healthy status in an expressive way.

Another example is that of two persons, one of them knowing the meaning of fear, and the other is subjected to it and is really experiencing it.

Methods of Emphasis in This *Āyah*

In the above *āyah* (*an-Nisā* 65), notice how Allāh (T) emphasizes the obligation of obeying the Messenger (S) in several ways:

1. Starting with a Negation

First, He precedes the oath with the negation, **«But no, by your Lord ...»**

This style of starting a sentence with a negation when making an oath concerning a negated matter [1] is common in the language of the Arabs. For instance as-Ṣiddīq [Abū Bakr (R)] said:

> "No, by Allāh! He shall not turn around to one of
> Allāh's lions, who fought for Allāh and His
> Messenger, and give you his booty." [2]

---

1 In this case, their *Īmān* is what is being negated.

2 The occasion for saying this is the following: Qatādah (R) narrated that he was with

Examples of this style are very numerous in the Arabic poetry as in the following two example:

> "No, by your father [1], O daughter of the one from the tribe of ʿĀmir,
> People cannot claim that I ever run away (in the battlefield)."

> "No, by Allāh! One cannot find for what ails me,
> Or what ails them - ever- a cure."

If you examine the sentences in the *Qurʾān* which include oaths, and which start with negation articles, you will find in most of them that the thing about which the oath is made is itself negated as well. This general rule is not revoked by Allāh's saying:

﴿فَلَا أُقْسِمُ بِمَوَاقِعِ ٱلنُّجُومِ، وَإِنَّهُ لَقَسَمٌ لَوْ تَعْلَمُونَ عَظِيمٌ. إِنَّهُ لَقُرْآنٌ كَرِيمٌ﴾ الواقعة ٧٥-٧٧

«But no! I swear by the setting of the stars - and verily, that is indeed a great oath, if you but know - that this is indeed a most honorable *Qurʾān*, in a Book well guarded (with Allāh)»[2]

The intention in these *āyāt* is to first negate the fallacies of the disbelievers regarding the *Qurʾān*: that it is poetry, magic, or fables of the past. Then they confirm the opposite. Thus they tell them, "But no!

Allāh's Messenger in the battle of Ḥunayn. When the *Muslims* approached victory, he saw a man of the disbelievers about to kill a *Muslim*. He ran to him from behind and hit him with the sword between the shoulders. The disbeliever turned around to Qatādah, held him, and squeezed him so hard that he felt he was about to die. But then, death came to him (because of Qatādah's hit), and he let go of him.

After the battle was over, the Prophet (S) said three times, ‹**Whoever kills an enemy and has a proof of it then he has the right to his booty.**›

Qatādah asked if anyone would testify before the Prophet (S) that he killed that man. A man then stood up and said, "He is saying the truth, O Messenger of Allāh; and I have taken his booty; so give him something to satisfy him instead."

Then Abū Bakr (R) said, "No, by Allāh! He shall not turn around to one of Allāh's lions, who fought for Allāh and His Messenger, and give you his booty." The Messenger (S) responded by saying, ‹**He is right! So give him [his booty].**› And he gave it to him. [Recorded by Al-Bukhārī and Muslim]

1 As explained in a footnote below, swearing by the fathers is prohibited in *Islām*.

2 *Al-Wāqiʿah* 57:75-78.

It is not what you claim, but is rather an honorable *Qur'ān*".

In other places, Allāh (T) explicitly mentions both the negation (underlined) and the affirmation (double underlined). For example, He (T) says:

﴿فَلَا أُقْسِمُ بِالْخُنَّسِ، الْجَوَارِ الْكُنَّسِ، وَاللَّيْلِ إِذَا عَسْعَسَ، وَالصُّبْحِ
إِذَا تَنَفَّسَ. إِنَّهُ لَقَوْلُ رَسُولٍ كَرِيمٍ، ذِي قُوَّةٍ عِنْدَ ذِي الْعَرْشِ
مَكِينٍ، مُطَاعٍ ثَمَّ أَمِينٍ. وَمَا صَاحِبُكُمْ بِمَجْنُونٍ، وَلَقَدْ رَآهُ بِالْأُفُقِ
الْمُبِينِ، وَمَا هُوَ عَلَى الْغَيْبِ بِضَنِينٍ، وَمَا هُوَ بِقَوْلِ شَيْطَانٍ رَجِيمٍ﴾
التكوير ١٥-٢٥

«But no! I swear by the planets that disappear during the day, running in their courses in secret, and the night as it departs, and the dawn as it brightens. Verily this (the *Qur'ān*) is the words (brought) by a most honorable messenger (Jibrīl), endowed with power and with rank before the Lord of the Throne (Allāh), obeyed (by the angels), trustworthy therein (in the heavens). People! Your companion (Muhammad) is not a madman; indeed he saw him (Jibrīl) in the clear horizon; and he does not withhold (from you) a knowledge of the *ghayb* [1] and it (the *Qur'ān*) is not the word of an outcast devil.» [2]

And:

﴿لَا أُقْسِمُ بِيَوْمِ الْقِيَامَةِ، وَلَا أُقْسِمُ بِالنَّفْسِ اللَّوَّامَةِ. أَيَحْسَبُ الْإِنْسَانُ
أَلَّنْ نَجْمَعَ عِظَامَهُ، بَلَى قَادِرِينَ عَلَى أَنْ نُسَوِّيَ بَنَانَهُ﴾ القيامة ١-٤

«But no! I do swear by the Day of Resurrection, and I swear by the self-reproaching soul (of a believer). Does the human being think that We

1 *Ghayb*: Domains beyond the human senses. This is commonly and erroneously translated as "the Unseen". It is used in the *Qur'ān* to denote all those sectors or phrases of reality which lie beyond the range of human perception: as, for instance, Allāh's existence, His attributes, the Hereafter, the angels, and unrecorded events of the remote past or future.

2 *At-Takwīr* 81:15-25.

shall not assemble his bones? Yes, We are Able to put together in perfect order the tips of his fingers.»[1]

Therefore, opening the oath with articles of negation emphasizes the matter being discussed, and confirms the absence of false claims or erroneous beliefs regarding it.

2. Using an Oath

The second method of emphasis is that Allāh (T) used an oath [to negate *Īmān* from those who do not fulfill the conditions of submitting to the Prophet's judgment as set forth in the rest of the *āyah*].

3. Swearing by Himself

The third method is that Allāh (T) chose to swear by Himself and not by any of His creatures, which He does on some occasions [2].

4. Requiring the Absence of Any Resistance

The fourth method of emphasis is that Allāh (T) requires submission to the Messenger's judgment, such that no resistance to it remains in the souls.

5. Complete Submission

And the fifth method of emphasis is in repeating the verb "submit" in the abstract form. Literally, this would be stated as: "... And submit a submission." In Arabic, this reflects the meaning: "... And submit completely or fully".

---

1 *Al-Qiyāmah* 75:1-4.

2 People, however, may only swear by Allāh (T), His Names, or His Attributes. The Messenger (S) instructed that anyone who wants to make an oath, should either make it by Allāh (T) or remain silent. [Al-Bukhārī and Muslim]

The Prophet's Claim on the Believers

The eloquent methods of emphasis applied here, and the great care taken to confirm this in the souls of the worshipers, are because of the great need of this important matter. Allāh (T) said:

﴿ٱلنَّبِيُّ أَوْلَىٰ بِٱلْمُؤْمِنِينَ مِنْ أَنفُسِهِمْ﴾ الأحزاب ٦

> **«The Prophet has a higher claim [1] on the believers than [they have on] their own selves.»** [2]

Some people think that the Messenger (S) cannot have more claim on them than their own selves. This *āyah* indicates that anyone who thinks like this is not one of the believers.

This Prophet's claim on the believers involves the following two important matters:

1. Dearer Than One's Self

The Messenger (S) should be more beloved than one's own self. This is so because the Prophet's claim on a believer is based on love; and a person usually loves himself more than others; yet the Messenger (S) should have more claim on him, and be dearer to him than himself. A person who fulfills this acquires the quality of *Īmān*.

Once a person submits to the Prophet's claim on him and loves him more than any other creature, then there follows full compliance, obedience, and all the other consequences of love, such as satisfaction with his judgment, submission to his orders, and favoring him over anyone else.

2. The Ruler over One's Self

A person should not have an independent rule over himself; this authority is the right of the Messenger (S). His rule is superior to a master's rule over his slave or a father's over his son. Thus, a person has no right of disposal over himself except in accordance with what the

---

1 The Arabic word used here is *awlā* which means that he (S) has more right and claim on a person. It also carries the meaning of closeness, i.e., that he (S) must be closer to a person than his own self. Some translations use this latter meaning, and we use it sometimes in this text.

2 *Al-Aḥzāb* 33:6.

Messenger (S) disposes, for he (S) has more claim on him than himself.

Deviation from the True Love

How then could such a closeness (to the Messenger) ever be attained by a person who isolates the Messenger's message from the position of authority [over himself and his life], who is more satisfied and pleased with someone else's judgment, who claims that the guidance is not acquired from him (S) but from the dictates of the minds, and who claims that the Messenger's message does not offer full certainty? These and other similar views reflect a deviation from him (S) and from his Message, and that indeed is the worst misguidance.

There is no way to establish the closeness to the Messenger (S) except by isolating oneself from all but him (S), following him in everything, and checking what anyone else says against that with which he (S) came. So, if the Messenger's testimony supports it, it is accepted, and if it invalidates it, it is rejected; and if it were unclear whether his testimony is for or against it then it is treated as the talk of the People of the Scripture, and no decision is made concerning it until he is sure which of the two judgments is closer to it.

The one who follows this method will have his journey of *hijrah* straightforward, his knowledge and deeds will be upright, and the people will aspire to him from every direction.

CHAPTER 4

JUSTICE AND FAIR TESTIMONY

Establishing Justice

It is surprising to find someone claiming closeness to the Messenger (S) and complete love for him while he strives to follow and establish someone else's opinions. He bases his anger, love, and satisfaction on such opinions; he referees them; and he compares the Messenger's statements to them - if they agree with those opinions then he accepts them, otherwise he applies all sorts of tricks and takes all measures to reject them and to turn away from them.

Allāh (T) said:

﴿يَا أَيُّهَا ٱلَّذِينَ آمَنُوا كُونُوا قَوَّامِينَ بِٱلْقِسْطِ شُهَدَاءَ لِلَّهِ وَلَوْ عَلَى أَنْفُسِكُمْ أَوِ ٱلْوَالِدَيْنِ وَٱلْأَقْرَبِينَ، إِنْ يَكُنْ غَنِيًّا أَوْ فَقِيرًا فَٱللَّهُ أَوْلَى بِهِمَا، فَلَا تَتَّبِعُوا ٱلْهَوَى أَنْ تَعْدِلُوا. وَإِنْ تَلْوُوا أَوْ تُعْرِضُوا فَإِنَّ ٱللَّهَ كَانَ بِمَا تَعْمَلُونَ خَبِيرًا﴾ النساء ١٣٥

«Believers! Stand out firmly for fair dealings, as witnesses to Allāh, even though it be against yourselves, or your parents, or your kin; be he rich or poor, Allāh can best protect both. So follow not the lusts [of your hearts] lest you may avoid justice. If you distort your testimony or refuse to provide it, verily, Allāh is ever Well-Acquainted with what you do.»[1]

This *āyah* carries great meanings that should be emphasized because of people's dire need for them.

Allāh (T) commands the believers to establish equity and justice. It should be rendered toward everyone, whether enemy or friend.

It is even more important to establish justice in matters of ideas, opinions, and beliefs, because they relate to Allāh's commands and teachings. Allowing whims and disobedience to influence one's opinions and beliefs conflicts with Allāh's commands and with His Messenger's Message.

Establishing justice in ideas, opinions and beliefs is the mission of

---

1 *An-Nisā'* 4:135.

the successors to the Messenger (S) in his *Ummah*[1] - those who are worthy of carrying the trust among his followers. No one deserves such description of honesty except those who establish absolute justice in this, as an advice for Allāh, His Book, His Messenger, and His worshipers. These are indeed the true inheritors [of the glorious Message]

Thus a person is not worthy of this description if he takes his company, ways, and opinions as measures and indicators of the truth - loathing or befriending people because of them.

How far is such a person from establishing the justice that Allāh mandated on everyone, especially in these matters of belief where the obligation is higher!

Fair Testimonies

The above *āyah* has, **«... as witnesses to Allāh ...»**. A witness is a reporter. If he reports truthfully then he is acceptable and just; if he reports falsehoods then he is a false witness.

In addition to establishing justice, Allāh requires one to be a witness for Him alone. Thus the testimony should be: with justice and for Allāh alone. In another *āyah* Allāh (T) said:

﴿يَا أَيُّهَا ٱلَّذِينَ آمَنُوا كُونُوا قَوَّامِينَ لِلهِ شُهَدَاءَ بِٱلْقِسْطِ﴾ المائدة ٨

«Believers! Stand out firmly for Allāh as witnesses to fair dealing.» [2]

Together, these two *āyāt* require four things: establishing justice, doing it for Allāh, maintaining truthful testimonies, and doing this for Allāh as well.

The *āyah* in *sūrat* [3] *an-Nisā* emphasizes fairness and maintaining the testimonies for Allāh, while that of *sūrat al-Mā'idah* emphasizes standing out firmly for Allāh and maintaining fair testimonies. This difference (between the two *āyāt*) has an important reason that cannot be dealt with here.

---

1 *Ummah*: Nation. It sometimes refers to all *Muslims*.

2 *Al-Mā'idah* 5:8.

3 *Sūrah* or *Sūrat*: A chapter of the *Qur'ān*.

THE TEST OF FAIRNESS

The above *āyah* (*an-Nisā' 135*) then says, **«... even if it be against your own selves, your parents or your kin ...».**

Allāh (T) commands to establish justice and to maintain fair testimony against everyone, including the most beloved ones. One is required to be fair against himself, his parents who are his roots, and his relatives who are usually closer and better supporters for him than other people.

A person's love for himself, his parents, and his kin, tends to prevent him from establishing the right and justice against them, especially when the right is for someone whom he hates and loathes. Thus, it is obvious that no one will establish this justice except he to whom Allāh (T) and His Messenger (S) are more beloved than anything else.

One can use this to test the strength of *Īmān* in his heart, and his status of *Īmān*.

On the other end, one should be just toward his enemies and those whom he dislikes. His hatred should not cause him to be unjust to them, just as his love for himself and his kin should not prevent him from establishing justice against them. This hatred should not make him do wrong, just as that love should not stop him from doing right. One of the *salaf* [1] said:

> "A just person is one whose anger does not cause him to do wrong, and whose pleasure does not prevent him from doing right."

Thus these two *āyāt* (of *an-Nisā'* and *al-Mā'idah*) together require two things: establishing justice, and maintaining fair testimony with friends and enemies.

WEALTH-BASED BIAS

The above *āyah* (*an-Nisā' 135*) then says, **«... be he rich or poor, Allāh is closer to both of them ...».**

[The meaning of this is that,] "Allāh is the Lord and Master of both the rich and the poor; they are His *'abid* (subjects), just as you are his *'abd*. So, do not be prejudiced toward a rich man because of his wealth, nor toward a poor man because of his poverty; Allāh (T) is closer than you to both of them."

1 *Salaf*: The early pious *Muslims* of the *Ṣaḥābah* and their true followers.

A possibly better interpretation of this is the following: "People may be reluctant to establish justice and to testify against the rich or the poor; as for the rich, they fear to cause him a loss in wealth; and as for the poor, they tend to take the matter lightly with him because of his poverty and that he possesses nothing. So they are told, 'Allāh is closer than you to both the rich and the poor; He is more knowledgeable of, and more merciful toward both; thus do not stop establishing truthful testimony against either of them.'"

Two Motivations for Hiding the Truth

The next portion of the above *āyah* (*an-Nisa' 135*) says, **«... so do not follow the lusts, lest you may be reluctant to establish justice ...».**

Another possible (but not as strong) interpretation of this *āyah* says, **«... lest you may be unjust ...»**

This *āyah* (*an-Nisa' 135*) continues, **«... if you distort your testimony, or refuse to provide it, verily, Allāh is ever Well-Acquainted with what you do.»**

Allāh (T) mentions here the two incentives for hiding the truth, warning against committing either of them. These are: distorting the testimony and refusing to provide it.

When the truth becomes clear and evident, a person who likes to hide it does so in one of two ways: he either turns away from it and abstains from mentioning it, acting by this as a mute devil, or he changes and distorts it.

The distortion of truth is either in words or in meaning. Distorting the words is done by adding, dropping, or replacing them with other words. It can also be done by uttering other words in such a way as to make the listener think that he heard something different from what was actually meant. This is similar to what the Jews did in greeting the Messenger (S) or on some other occasions [1].

Distorting the meaning is done by interpreting the words differently from what the speaker intended, introducing that which he did not mean, dropping some of what he meant, and so on.

Summary

Thus Allāh (T) warns against all kinds of distortion in the testimony. A

1 When greeting the Messenger (S), some Jews used to fake "*As-Salāmu 'Alaykum*" (Peace be on you) by saying "*As-Sāmmu 'Alaykum*" (Death be to you) instead [Al-Bukhārī and Muslim]. Also, review *al-Mujādalah* 58:8.

witness is required to provide a precise testimony, without hiding or distorting it.

Just contemplate then on the great amount of wisdom and knowledge contained in this *āyah*.

In summary, *Īmān* is not complete, or not even present in a person, unless he submits the Texts [of the *Qur'ān* and *Sunnah*] with acceptance and pleasure, proclaims them, and invites people to them. He should never respond to them with rejection or distortion.

CHAPTER 5

OBEYING THE MESSENGER

Decisions of Allāh and His Messenger

Allāh (T) said:

﴿وَمَا كَانَ لِمُؤْمِنٍ وَلَا مُؤْمِنَةٍ إِذَا قَضَى ٱللهُ وَرَسُولُهُ أَمْرًا أَن يَكُونَ
لَهُمُ ٱلْخِيَرَةُ مِنْ أَمْرِهِمْ﴾ الأحزاب ٣٦

> **«It is not befitting for a believing man or woman, when a matter has been decided by Allāh and His Messenger, to have any option about their decision.»** [1]

This *āyah* indicates that when it is confirmed that Allāh (T) or His Messenger (S) have made a decision or have informed about a particular matter, then no believer, male or female, may choose differently. Any opposing choice would contradict *Īmān*.

Ash-Shāfi'ī (r) reported a consensus among the scholars of the *Ṣaḥābah*, the *Tābi'īn*, and their followers, that:

> "If a *sunnah* of Allāh's Messenger (S) becomes manifest to a person, he does not have any choice but to follow it, regardless of what other people say."

No *Muslim* scholar disputes doubts the truth of this statement. The only evidence that people are required to follow [beside Allāh's Book] is the words of the Infallible (Muḥammad (S)) who **«... does not say anything out of (his own) desire.»** [2]

Other people's talks could, at best, be acceptable to follow. But in no way may they oppose or outweigh the Texts (of the *Qur'ān* and *Sunnah*). We ask Allāh (T) to protect us from the failure [incurred on those who do not abide by this].

---

1 *Al-Aḥzāb* 33:36.

2 *An-Najm* 53:3.

The Guidance Is in Obeying the Messenger

Also, Allāh (T) said:

﴿قُلْ أَطِيعُوا ٱللهَ وَأَطِيعُوا ٱلرَّسُولَ، فَإِنْ تَوَلَّوْا فَإِنَّمَا عَلَيْهِ مَا حُمِّلَ وَعَلَيْكُمْ مَا حُمِّلْتُمْ، وَإِنْ تُطِيعُوهُ تَهْتَدُوا، وَمَا عَلَى ٱلرَّسُولِ إِلَّا ٱلْبَلَاغُ ٱلْمُبِينُ﴾ النور ٥٤

«Say: "Obey Allāh and obey the Messenger: but if you turn away then he (the Messenger) is only responsible for the duty placed on him, and you for that placed on you. If you obey him, you shall be on right guidance. The Messenger's duty is only clear deliverance [of the Message]".»[1]

Note that repeating the verb "obey" here has an important significance that will be discussed below.

Here Allāh (T) makes obeying the Messenger (S) a condition for guidance; guidance cannot be acquired without this obedience. The duty of the Messenger (S) is to deliver the Message; and people's duty is to follow, obey, and submit to him. Al-Bukhārī (r) reported that Az-Zuhrī [2] said:

> "From Allāh [comes] the knowledge; from the Messenger (S) [comes] the deliverance [of the knowledge]; and from us [comes] the submission [to the Message]."

Thus if people neglect their duty of belief and obedience, they would harm themselves not him; his responsibility is not to make them believe, but only to deliver the Message to them; it is not required from him that people be guided and successful.

Addressing the Believers

And Allāh (T) said:

﴿يَا أَيُّهَا ٱلَّذِينَ آمَنُوا أَطِيعُوا ٱللهَ وَأَطِيعُوا ٱلرَّسُولَ وَأُولِي ٱلْأَمْرِ

1 *An-Nūr* 24:54.

2 One of the *Tābi'īn*. He is a famous scholar of *Ḥadīth* and one of the important teachers of al-Bukhārī.

مِنكُمْ، فَإِن تَنَازَعْتُمْ فِي شَيْءٍ فَرُدُّوهُ إِلَى ٱللَّهِ وَٱلرَّسُولِ إِن كُنتُمْ تُؤْمِنُونَ بِٱللَّهِ وَٱلْيَوْمِ ٱلْآخِرِ. ذَٰلِكَ خَيْرٌ وَأَحْسَنُ تَأْوِيلاً﴾ النساء ٥٩

«Believers! Obey Allāh, and obey the Messenger and those charged with authority among you; if you differ in anything, refer it to Allāh and the Messenger (for judgment) if you (truly) believe in Allāh and the Last Day: that is best, and most suitable for final determination.»[1]

Allāh (T) is requiring obedience to Him and to His Messenger (S). He starts the *āyah* with an address to the "believers", hinting that what is required thereafter is a consequence of that name with which they are addressed.

This is similar to saying, "You whom Allāh has favored and enriched with His bounties, be good to others as Allāh has been good to you." And like, "Learned man, teach people what would benefit them." And, "Ruler, rule with justice." And so on.

For this reason, legislative matters in the *Qur'ān* are frequently addressed to the believers, starting the address with "Believers". For example Allāh says:

﴿يَا أَيُّهَا ٱلَّذِينَ آمَنُوا كُتِبَ عَلَيْكُمُ ٱلصِّيَامُ﴾ البقرة ١٨٣

«Believers, fasting is prescribed for you.» [2]

And He says:

﴿يَا أَيُّهَا ٱلَّذِينَ آمَنُوا إِذَا نُودِيَ لِلصَّلَاةِ مِن يَوْمِ ٱلْجُمُعَةِ فَٱسْعَوْا إِلَى ذِكْرِ ٱللَّهِ﴾ الجمعة ٩

«Believer, when the call is proclaimed for prayer on Friday, hasten earnestly to the remembrance of Allāh.» [3]

And He says:

﴿يَا أَيُّهَا ٱلَّذِينَ آمَنُوا أَوْفُوا بِٱلْعُقُودِ﴾ المائدة ١

«Believers, fulfill the contracts.»[4]

---

1 *An-Nisā'* 4:59.

2 *Al-Baqarah* 2:183.

3 *Al-Jumu'ah* 62:9.

4 *Al-Mā'idah* 5:1.

Addressing the believers like this carries the implication that: "If you are true believers, you should perform the following action, because it is a requirement for the integrity and sincerity of *Īmān*."

To Obey the Messenger Is to Obey Allāh

In the above *āyah* (*an-Nisā'* 59), Allāh demands obedience to Him, the Messenger, and those of authority. The verb "obey" is applied only once in regard to the Messenger and those of authority. One might expect the opposite - [that it would be applied only once in regard to both Allāh and the Messenger] because:

﴿مَنْ يُطِعِ ٱلرَّسُولَ فَقَدْ أَطَاعَ ٱللَّهَ﴾ النساء ٨٠

> **«He who obeys the Messenger obeys Allāh indeed.»** [1]

However, this usage here has a subtle meaning. It implies that the Messenger must be obeyed in all that he commands, even if it were not something specifically required in *Qur'ān*.

Let one then not imagine that the Messenger (S) should only be obeyed when his commands confirm the *Qur'ān*, otherwise he need not be obeyed. [In refutation of such fallacy, al-Miqdām bin Ma'di Yakrib (R) narrated that] he (S) said :

> **‹There will be a man with full stomach, reclining on his pillow, who will hear a command from me and say, "Let the judge between us (in this matter) be Allāh's Book: we obey whatever we find in it." [Know that] indeed, I have been given the Book and, with it, that which is similar to it (the *Sunnah*).›** [2]

However, obeying the people of authority is not required independently, but as part of obeying the Messenger (S). This fact is confirmed by the *ḥadīth* (narrated by Ibn 'Umar (R)):

> **‹One should listen and obey (those charged with authority) whether it were something he liked or**

---

1 *An-Nisā'* 4:80.

2 Recorded by Aḥmad, Abū Dāwūd, and others; judged authentic by al-Albānī (*Saḥīḥ ul-Jāmi'* no. 2640).

hated, as long as he is not commanded to disobey Allāh (T). If he is commanded to disobey Allāh, he should neither listen nor obey.› [1]

Toward the end of this *āyah* (*an-Nisā'* 59), Allāh emphasizes obeying the Messenger (S) by saying (what means), **«... refer it to Allāh** **and the** **Messenger ...»** rather than saying, "... and to the Messenger ...". Referring matters to the *Qur'ān* is equivalent to referring them to Allāh and the Messenger. Also, Allāh's judgement is the same as His Messenger's; and the Messenger's judgment is the same as Allāh's.

Thus if you refer your disputes to Allāh, i.e. to His Book, then you refer to His Messenger (S) as well. And if you refer to His Messenger (S), then you refer to Allāh as well. This is one of the subtleties of the *Qur'ān*.

The People of Authority

Two views have been expressed by the *Ṣaḥābah* and the *'ulamā'* as to who are the ones "charged with authority". The first is that they are the *'ulamā'*, and the other is that they are the rulers.

In reality, it applies to both groups, because both the *'ulamā'* and the rulers are in charge of the affairs concerning which Allāh has sent His Messenger.

As for the *'ulamā'*, they are charged with protecting the *Dīn*, explaining it, teaching it, and refuting those who deviate from it or try to alter it. Allāh (T) gave them this charge, as He said:

﴿أُوْلَئِكَ الَّذِينَ آتَيْنَاهُمُ الْكِتَابَ وَالْحُكْمَ وَالنُّبُوَّةَ، فَإِن يَكْفُرْ بِهَا هَؤُلاَءِ
فَقَدْ وَكَّلْنَا بِهَا قَوْمًا لَيْسُوا بِهَا بِكَافِرِينَ﴾ الأنعام ٨٩

«These [prophets] were the men to whom We granted the Book and Judgement and Prophethood; if these people [of the Scripture] reject them, behold! We shall entrust their charge to a new people who do not reject them.» [2]

This is indeed a great assignment to the *'ulamā'* that requires from people to obey and follow them.

And as for the rulers, they are charged with establishing the *Dīn*,

1 Recorded by al-Bukhārī and Muslim.
2 *Al-An'ām* 6:89.

safeguarding it, compelling people to adhere to it, and punishing those who deviate from it.

Thus these two groups are in charge of the affairs of people, and other people are their followers and subjects.

Matters of Dispute

Furthermore, there is in the above *āyah* (*an-Nisā'* 59) a clear evidence that all matters of disagreement, in all aspects of the *Dīn*, should be referred to Allāh and His Messenger (S) - and to no one else.

Anyone referring disputes to other than Allāh and His Messenger opposes this command by Allāh. And anyone who calls to other than Allāh's and His Messenger's judgment to resolve disagreements, calls indeed with the call of *Jāhiliyyah*[1].

One does not truly enter the realm of *Īmān* until he refers all differences arising among people to Allāh and His Messenger. For this reason, this *āyah* continues as, **«... if you believe in Allāh and the Last Day ...»**

Thus if this condition (of referring disputes to Allāh and His Messenger) is not satisfied by a person, this implies the absence of *Īmān* in him.

This *āyah* should be a sufficient clarification and guidance in this matter (of obeying the Messenger). It constitutes a protection and a support for those who abide by it; and it is a powerful refutation and attack against those who deny it, as Allāh (T) said:

﴿لِيَهْلِكَ مَنْ هَلَكَ عَنْ بَيِّنَةٍ وَيَحْيَىٰ مَنْ حَيَّ عَنْ بَيِّنَةٍ، وَإِنَّ اللهَ لَسَمِيعٌ عَلِيمٌ﴾ الأنفال ٤٢

> **«... That he who would perish might perish in clear evidence [of the truth], and that he who would remain alive might live in clear evidence [of the truth]. And verily Allāh is All-Hearing, All-Knowing.»**[2]

The earlier and later *Muslims* agreed that referring matters to Allāh means referring them to His Book, and referring matters to the Messenger (S) means referring them to him personally during his life, and to his *Sunnah* after his death.

---

1 *Jāhiliyyah*: The state of ignorance and disbelief which prevailed in the Arab Peninsula before *Islām*.

2 *Al-Anfāl* 8:42.

The Excellence of Obeying the Messenger

The above *āyah* (*an-Nisā'* 59) ends with, **«... that is best, and most suitable for final determination.»** This means, "That with which I commanded you (to obey Me and obey My Messenger and the people of authority, and to refer disputes to Me and My Messenger) is better for you in this life and in the Hereafter; it leads to your happiness in both lives. Therefore, it is best and most rewarding for you."

This indicates that obeying Allāh (T) and His Messenger (S), and taking them as the referees, is the means to immediate and continued happiness.

Anyone who examines closely the evils of the world will find that each of them is caused by disobeying the Messenger (S). Similarly, every good in the world results from obeying him. Furthermore, all the evils and pains in the Hereafter result from disobeying him (S).

Thus, all the evils in both lives are caused by disobeying the Messenger (S) and by its consequences. If people obeyed him (S) properly, there would be no evil on earth. This applies equally to the general natural catastrophes and calamities, and to the personal evils, pains, and sorrow that occur to people.

In obeying him (S) is a refuge and a protection for those who want to prosper and be happy. And this prosperity and happiness cannot be achieved until one strives first to learn what the Messenger (S) taught, and then confirm it with true actions.

The Human Excellence

There are two additional actions which complete the happiness arising from truly obeying the Messenger (S). The first is to invite people to obey him (S), and the second is to have patience and perseverance in fulfilling this mission.

Thus the human excellence is confined to four matters:

First, knowing the Message of Messenger (S).
Second, acting in accordance with this knowledge.
Third, spreading this knowledge among people and inviting them to it.
Fourth, persevering and striving in accomplishing all this.

One who seeks to learn how the *Ṣaḥābah* (R) lived and who want to follow them should know that this was indeed their way [so let him follow it]. A poet once said:

"If you want to reach those folk, follow their way:
It is quite manifest for those who aspire to it."

CHAPTER 6
THE PEOPLE OF MISERY

Deviating from the Messenger

Allāh (T) said addressing His Messenger (S):

﴿قُلْ إِنْ ضَلَلْتُ فَإِنَّمَا أَضِلُّ عَلَى نَفْسِي، وَإِنِ ٱهْتَدَيْتُ فَبِمَا يُوحِي إِلَيَّ رَبِّي، إِنَّهُ سَمِيعٌ قَرِيبٌ﴾ سبأ ٥٠

«Say, "Were I to go astray, I would only stray to the hurt of myself; but if I am guided, it is because of what my Lord reveals unto me; He is indeed All-Hearing, Ever-Near."» [1]

This carries a clear evidence that the Messenger's guidance occurs only through the *waḥy* [2]. How surprising it is then to find men with confused minds and conflicting opinions claim to be guided! How does this guidance reach them? Indeed, **«He whom Allāh guides is rightly guided; but as for him whom He leaves to stray, you will find no protector to lead him.»** [3]

What misguidance is worse than that of one who claims that guidance does not occur through the *waḥy*! He would rather refer matters to the opinions of this and that person! Great indeed is Allāh's bounty toward one whom He guarded from such a serious deviation and a great disaster. All praise is due to Allāh, Lord of the peoples.

FOLLOWING FALSEHOODS

Also, Allāh (T) said:

﴿كِتَابٌ أُنْزِلَ إِلَيْكَ فَلَا يَكُنْ فِي صَدْرِكَ حَرَجٌ مِنْهُ لِتُنْذِرَ بِهِ وَذِكْرَى لِلْمُؤْمِنِينَ * ٱتَّبِعُوا مَا أُنْزِلَ إِلَيْكُمْ مِنْ رَبِّكُمْ وَلَا تَتَّبِعُوا مِنْ دُونِهِ أَوْلِيَاءَ، قَلِيلاً مَا تَذَكَّرُونَ﴾ الأعراف ٢-٣

1 *Saba'* 34:50.

2 *Waḥy*: The revelation.

3 *Al-Kahf* 18:17.

«A Book has been revealed unto you, so let there be no tightness in your chest about it - that you might warn [people] with it, and remind the Believers. Follow [people] what has been sent down to you from your Lord, and do not follow other than Him - as allies or protectors. How seldom do you remember [the admonition].» [1]

Here, Allāh (T) commands people to follow what He revealed to His Messenger, and He forbids following others. One can either follow the Revelation or follow others - as allies; Allāh does not give other than these two alternatives. Thus, anyone not following the *waḥy* is indeed following falsehoods and other allies instead of Allāh. By Allāh's Grace, this should be clear and obvious.

The Confidants

And Allāh (T) said:

﴿وَيَوْمَ يَعَضُّ ٱلظَّالِمُ عَلَى يَدَيْهِ، يَقُولُ: يَا لَيْتَنِي ٱتَّخَذْتُ مَعَ ٱلرَّسُولِ سَبِيلاً، يَا وَيْلَتَىٰ، لَيْتَنِي لَمْ أَتَّخِذْ فُلَاناً خَلِيلاً. لَقَدْ أَضَلَّنِي عَنِ ٱلذِّكْرِ بَعْدَ إِذْ جَاءَنِي. وَكَانَ ٱلشَّيْطَانُ لِلْإِنْسَانِ خَذُولاً﴾ الفرقان ٢٧-٢٩

«On the Day when the wrong-doer will bite his hands [in despair], saying, "Oh! Would that I had followed the path shown to me by the Messenger! Ah! Woe is me! Would that I had never taken so-and-so for a confidant! Indeed, he lead me astray from the Message (of Allāh) after it had come to me! Ah! Satan is ever a betrayer of man."» [2]

Anyone who follows a person other than the Messenger (S), abandoning his guidance for the sake of that person's words or opinions, will surely say these same words. This is why Allāh refers here to the confidant as 'so-and-so', which is a generic term that could apply to any person taken as a confidant instead of Allāh.

This applies then to confidants whose friendship is based on anything other than obeying the Messenger (S): their friendship will

1 *Al-Aʿrāf* 7:2-3.

2 *Al-Furqān* 25:27-29.

eventually turn to enmity and accusations, as Allāh (T) said:

﴿ٱلْأَخِلَّاءُ يَوْمَئِذٍ بَعْضُهُمْ لِبَعْضٍ عَدُوٌّ، إِلَّا ٱلْمُتَّقِينَ﴾ الزخرف ٦٧

«The confidants on that Day will be foes unto one another - except the pious.» [1]

THE FOLLOWERS AND THE FOLLOWED

Allāh (T) describes the plight of the followers and of those whom they followed in several places of His Book; He says for instance:

﴿يَوْمَ تُقَلَّبُ وُجُوهُهُمْ فِي ٱلنَّارِ، يَقُولُونَ يَا لَيْتَنَا أَطَعْنَا ٱللهَ وَأَطَعْنَا
ٱلرَّسُولَاْ. وَقَالُوا رَبَّنَا إِنَّا أَطَعْنَا سَادَتَنَا وَكُبَرَاءَنَا فَأَضَلُّونَا ٱلسَّبِيلَاْ.
رَبَّنَا آتِهِمْ ضِعْفَيْنِ مِنَ ٱلْعَذَابِ وَٱلْعَنْهُمْ لَعْنًا كَبِيرًا﴾ الأحزاب ٦٦-٦٨

«On the Day when their faces will be tossed about in the Fire, they will say, "Woe to us! Would that we had obeyed Allāh and obeyed the Messenger!" And they will say, "Our Lord! We obeyed our chiefs and our great men, and they lead us astray from the right path. Our Lord! Give them double suffering, and banish them utterly from Your Grace!"» [2]

Those people will wish that they had obeyed Allāh (T) and His Messenger (S). But they will do it at a time when wishes avail them nothing. They will confess that they had obeyed their chiefs and leaders and disobeyed the Messenger (S), acknowledging that they had no excuse for doing so. This realization will lead them to request doubling the punishment and curses for those leaders.

This carries an important lesson and a useful admonition for a man of reason. Indeed, assistance [in seeing the truth] is from Allāh (T) only.

---

1 *Az-Zukhruf* 43:67.

2 *Al-Aḥzāb* 33:66-68.

Partners in Deviation

Allāh (T) said,

﴿فَمَنْ أَظْلَمُ مِمَّنِ ٱفْتَرَىٰ عَلَى ٱللهِ كَذِبًا أَوْ كَذَّبَ بِآيَاتِهِ ، أُوْلَٰئِكَ
يَنَالُهُمْ نَصِيبُهُمْ مِنَ ٱلْكِتَابِ، حَتَّىٰ إِذَا جَاءَتْهُمْ رُسُلُنَا يَتَوَفَّوْنَهُمْ قَالُوا:
أَيْنَ مَا كُنتُمْ تَدْعُونَ مِنْ دُونِ ٱللهِ؟ قَالُوا: ضَلُّوا عَنَّا. وَشَهِدُوا عَلَىٰ
أَنْفُسِهِمْ أَنَّهُمْ كَانُوا كَافِرِينَ. قَالَ :ٱدْخُلُوا فِي أُمَمٍ قَدْ خَلَتْ مِنْ قَبْلِكُمْ
مِنَ ٱلْجِنِّ وَٱلْإِنْسِ فِي ٱلنَّارِ. كُلَّمَا دَخَلَتْ أُمَّةٌ لَعَنَتْ أُخْتَهَا، حَتَّىٰ
إِذَا ٱدَّارَكُوا فِيهَا جَمِيعًا قَالَتْ أُخْرَاهُمْ لِأُولَاهُمْ :رَبَّنَا هَٰؤُلَاءِ أَضَلُّونَا
فَآتِهِمْ عَذَابًا ضِعْفًا مِنَ ٱلنَّارِ. قَالَ: لِكُلٍّ ضِعْفٌ وَلَٰكِنْ لَا تَعْلَمُونَ .
وَقَالَتْ أُولَاهُمْ لِأُخْرَاهُمْ: فَمَا كَانَ لَكُمْ عَلَيْنَا مِنْ فَضْلٍ، فَذُوقُوا
ٱلْعَذَابَ بِمَا كُنتُمْ تَكْسِبُونَ﴾ الأعراف ٣٧-٣٩

«Who could be more unjust than one who devises lies against Allāh or rejects His messages? For such, their appointed portion must reach them from the Book [of Decrees] until, when Our messengers [of death] arrive to take their souls, they say, "Where are the things that you used to invoke besides Allāh?" They will reply, "They have forsaken us!" And thus they will testify against themselves that they had been denying the truth (*kāfirs*).

He (Allāh) will say, "Join those peoples who have preceded you, of men and *jinn* [1], in the Fire." Every time a new people enters, it curses its sister people [that went before].

Once they have all joined each other in it, the last of them will say about the first, "Our Lord! It is these who have misled us, so give them a double suffering in the Fire." He will reply, "Every one of you will have a double suffering, but this you do

1 *Jinn*: An invisible creation that Allāh (T) made from fire and smoke. Like human beings, the *jinns* have a choice of action, and are accountable for their deeds. Satan is one of the *jinns*.

not understand." Then the first of them will say to the last, "See then! You have no advantage over us, so taste of the suffering for all that you did!"» [1]

A sensible person should reflect on these *āyāt*, and on the lessons they carry.

The first *āyah* (*al-Aʿrāf* 37) mentions the two classes of evildoers:

a) Those who start fallacies, establish injustice, and call people to it. Thus they distort the truth and initiate falsehood.
b) Those who reject or deny the truth.

Every evildoer belongs to one of these two classes. If, in addition, he invites people to his evil and drives them away from the truth, then he deserves a double penalty because of his disbelief and evil. For this reason Allāh (T) says:

﴿ٱلَّذِينَ كَفَرُوا وَصَدُّوا عَن سَبِيلِ ٱللَّهِ زِدْنَاهُمْ عَذَابًا فَوْقَ ٱلْعَذَابِ بِمَا كَانُوا يُفْسِدُونَ﴾ النحل ٨٨

«Those who disbelieve and hinder people from the Path of Allāh, for them will We add penalty to penalty because of the mischief that they used to spread.» [2]

They deserve a double punishment because of their double evil. But as for those who commit *kufr* (disbelief) without coaxing others toward it, Allāh (T) does not threaten them with a doubled suffering:

﴿وَلِلْكَافِرِينَ عَذَابٌ أَلِيمٌ﴾ المجادلة ٤

«For those who disbelieve, there is a grievous punishment...» [3]

In the above *āyāt* (7:37-39), Allāh (T) informs that what had been decreed for the evildoers in their first life reaches them, such as their life span, sustenance, etc.

Then, when death comes to them, they part with their old claims, acknowledge their falsehood, and become witnesses against themselves.

Allāh (T) commands them to enter into the Fire where many previous peoples have preceded them. Every time a new people enters,

---

1 *Al-Aʿrāf* 7:37-39.
2 *An-Naḥl* 16:88.
3 *Al- Mujādalah* 58:4.

its members curse their ancestors who preceded them into the Fire. When they are all in it, the later nations request doubled penalties for the previous ones because they led them astray and drove them away from obeying Allāh's messengers.

Allāh (T) replies that the punishment will be doubled for both the "followers" and the "followed", in accordance with their deviation and disbelief, and that a generation does not know what doubled suffering other generations deserve.

The former generation then tells the later, "You do not possess any advantage over us. You had your own messengers who showed you the truth, warned you against our deviation, and forbade you from following or imitating us. Yet you rejected them and insisted on following and imitating us, and on forsaking the guidance of the messengers. Thus what advantage do you have over us, when you strayed just as we did, and when you gave up the truth just like us? You strayed because of us, just as we strayed because of other people. You can claim no advantage over us, and thus you should taste the suffering because of what you earned yourselves."

By Allāh, this is indeed a strong admonition and an eloquent advice for any living heart! These, and similar *āyāt* would awaken the hearts of those who migrate to Allāh (T). But as for the lazy people, they have no effect on them.

Untrue Followers

The above discussion deals with the followers who share in the deviation with those whom they follow.

Another case is that of the followers who turn away from whom they claim to follow, taking a different course than theirs, while maintaining false claims of true compliance with them. Allāh (T) mentions such people in the following:

﴿إِذْ تَبَرَّأَ ٱلَّذِينَ ٱتُّبِعُوا مِنَ ٱلَّذِينَ ٱتَّبَعُوا، وَرَأَوُا ٱلْعَذَابَ وَتَقَطَّعَتْ بِهِمُ ٱلْأَسْبَابُ. وَقَالَ ٱلَّذِينَ ٱتَّبَعُوا: لَوْ أَنَّ لَنَا كَرَّةً فَنَتَبَرَّأَ مِنْهُمْ كَمَا تَبَرَّؤُوا مِنَّا. كَذَٰلِكَ يُرِيهِمُ ٱللهُ أَعْمَالَهُمْ حَسَرَاتٍ عَلَيْهِمْ، وَمَا هُمْ بِخَارِجِينَ مِنَ ٱلنَّارِ﴾ البقرة ١٦٦-١٦٧

«Then would those who had been followed disown their followers; they (the followers) would see the suffering [awaiting them], and all relations

between them would be cut off. And then those followers would say: "If we can only have one more chance: we would disown them as they have disowned us." Thus will Allāh show them the fruits of their deeds as nothing but bitter regrets. Nor will there be a way for them out of the Fire.»[1]

The followed ones are truly guided. Their "followers" claim to adhere to them when, in reality, they follow a different way and guidance. They claim to love them, presuming that this love would benefit them despite their deviation. But they will discover on the Day of Judgement that they will be disowned by them. They take them as allies instead of Allāh, imagining this to benefit them!

Great indeed is the deviation of a person who takes other than Allāh (T) and His Messenger (S) for allies and confidants, making peace or hostility for their sake, and getting satisfied or infuriated for their cause. Regardless of how numerous his deeds are, or how much effort and toil he puts into them, they will be futile on the Day of Judgement, and will only add to his misery and regret.

His allegiance and enmity, love and hatred, satisfaction and anger, and so on, are not sincerely maintained for Allāh and His Messenger; because of this, Allāh will shatter his deeds and sever his connections.

The Only Un-severed Tie

Thus, on the Day of Resurrection, all connections and allegiances that had not been for Allāh will be severed, leaving only one tie: that which connects a *ʿabd* to his Lord.

This tie is maintained by:

a) Continued migration to Allāh and to His Messenger (S).
b) Continuously purifying one's acts of worship to Allāh (T). This includes love, hatred, giving, preventing, taking as allies or enemies, and the like.
c) Continuously purifying one's adherence to the Messenger (S). This includes abandoning others' opinions for what he says, discarding anything that disagrees with his guidance, and associating none with him in this adherence.

This is the only tie that will not be severed. It is the true

1 *Al-Baqarah* 2:166-167.

relationship between a *ʿabd* and his Lord: the relationship of pure *ʿubūdiyyah*. It is the only thing that he continues to long for, no matter how far he departs from it. It is as a poet once said:

> "Let your heart wander in love affairs as you wish:
> True love will only be for the first lover.
> How many houses does a man habituate!
> But he will always long for his first home."

This relationship [with Allāh] is the only one that profits man. Nothing else will profit him in any of his three lives: the first, the intermediate (*barzakh*), and the final eternal life. He cannot endure or live or be happy and successful without this relationship. A poet once said:

> "When ties (of communion) will be severed (between lovers),
> The bond of the true lovers [of Allāh] will not be possible to sever,
> And when their unity shatters,
> The unity of the true lovers [of Allāh] will be impossible to splinter."

Conclusion

In conclusion, on the Day of Judgement Allāh will sever all connections and ties that are among people in this life, sparing only the ties between them and Him - the ties that reflect pure *ʿubūdiyyah*, which can only be accomplished through true adherence to the messengers (S).

Allāh (T) said:

﴿وَقَدِمْنَا إِلَى مَا عَمِلُوا مِنْ عَمَلٍ فَجَعَلْنَاهُ هَبَاءً مَنْثُوراً﴾ الفرقان ٢٣

«And We shall turn to whatever deeds they did (in the first life), and We shall make such deeds as floating dust scattered about.» [1]

So all the deeds of the first life conflicting with the way and guidance of Allāh's messengers, and with which was sought anything other than Allāh's Countenance, will be turned by Allāh (on the Day of Judgement) into scattered dust, availing their owners nothing.

1 *Al-Furqān* 26:23.

This is indeed one of the greatest miseries on the Day of Judgement: for one to find all he did completely lost and worthless, at a time when one will be in the greatest need for every good deed.

CHAPTER 7
THE PEOPLE OF BLISS

Contrary to the miserable people discussed in the last chapter, our discussion will now focus on the people of happiness and bliss. These can be divided into two classes.

The First Class of Happy People

The first class consists of those who possess the quality of intellectual independence; they are described by Allāh (T) as follows:

﴿وَٱلسَّابِقُونَ ٱلْأَوَّلُونَ مِنَ ٱلْمُهَاجِرِينَ وَٱلْأَنْصَارِ وَٱلَّذِينَ ٱتَّبَعُوهُم بِإِحْسَانٍ رَضِيَ ٱللهُ عَنْهُمْ وَرَضُوا عَنْهُ﴾ التوبة ١٠٠

«The first and foremost [to embrace *Islām*] of the *Muhājirīn* [1] and the *Ansār* [2], and also those who follow them in the best way; Allāh is well-pleased with them, and they are with Him.» [3]

These are the happy ones for whom Allāh's acceptance is confirmed. They are the Companions of Allāh's Messenger (S) and those who follow them in the best way until the Day of Resurrection.

The conventional expression "*Tābi'ūn*" applies to the companions' followers who have met with them in person. However, the description here is not restricted to them, but includes anyone who righteously follows their way; and any such person is of those with whom Allāh (T) is pleased and who are also pleased with Him.

FOLLOWING WITH *IḤSĀN*

The manner of following the *Ṣaḥābah* (in this *āyah*) is not ambiguous.

---

1 *Muhājir*: A migrator - one who undertakes *hijrah*. Plural: *muhājirūn* or *muhājirīn*. Reference here is specifically to those who migrated from Makkah to al-Madīnah in obedience to Allāh.

2 *Anṣār*: Those who give help and aid. It usually refers to the citizens of al-Madīnah who gave aid to the *Muhājirīn* when they migrated to their town.

3 *At-Tawbah* 9:100.

It is restricted by Allāh (T) to being in the "best way". It cannot be fulfilled merely by wishes, or by adhering to them in some matters while rejecting them in others. It should always be done with *Iḥsān* (with righteousness and in the best way); this is a condition to deserve Allāh's (T) acceptance and His Gardens. He (T) said:

﴿هُوَ ٱلَّذِي بَعَثَ فِي ٱلْأُمِّيِّينَ رَسُولاً مِنْهُمْ يَتْلُو عَلَيْهِمْ آيَاتِهِ وَيُزَكِّيهِمْ
وَيُعَلِّمُهُمُ ٱلْكِتَابَ وَٱلْحِكْمَةَ، وَإِنْ كَانُوا مِنْ قَبْلُ لَفِي ضَلَالٍ مُبِينٍ.
وَآخَرِينَ مِنْهُمْ لَمَّا يَلْحَقُوا بِهِمْ، وَهُوَ ٱلْعَزِيزُ ٱلْحَكِيمُ. ذَٰلِكَ فَضْلُ ٱللهِ
يُؤْتِيهِ مَنْ يَشَاءُ، وَٱللهُ ذُو ٱلْفَضْلِ ٱلْعَظِيمِ﴾ الجمعة ٢-٤

«He it is Who has sent among the unlettered a messenger [Muḥammad] from among themselves, to convey unto them His messages, to sanctify them, and to instruct them in the Book and the Wisdom, although they had been before in manifest error. And He has sent him also to other people who have not quite reached them (the *Ṣaḥābah*); He is All-Mighty, All-Wise. That is the bounty of Allāh which He bestows on whom He will. Allāh is the One of great bounty.» [1]

The first group of people mentioned here are those who met the Messenger (S) and accompanied him. The latter are those who did not meet the first group; this applies to anyone who comes after them and adheres to their way, until the Day of Resurrection. This group falls behind the first group (the *Ṣaḥābah*) both in era and in stature, even though both groups are of the happy ones.

THREE KINDS OF HEARTS

A third group of people would be those who reject the Guidance that Allāh (T) sent with His Messenger (S), or who do not benefit from it. Those are described by Allāh (T) in the following:

﴿مَثَلُ ٱلَّذِينَ حُمِّلُوا ٱلتَّوْرَاةَ ثُمَّ لَمْ يَحْمِلُوهَا كَمَثَلِ ٱلْحِمَارِ يَحْمِلُ
أَسْفَاراً﴾ الجمعة ٥

1 *Al-Jumuʿah* 62:2-4.

«The likeness of those who were entrusted with the responsibility of the Torah, but who subsequently failed in that, is as the likeness of a donkey which carries a huge burden of books [but understands nothing of them]...» [1]

The Prophet (S) also classified people into three groups based on their response to his Message and Guidance. He said:

‹An example of the guidance and knowledge with which Allāh (T) has sent me is that of a rain that falls on different kinds of land:
1) One land is good; it accepts water and produces vegetation and grass in plenty.
2) Another land is dry with a solid bed that reserves water so that people can drink and irrigate with it.
3) The third kind is a porous land that can neither retain water nor produce vegetation.
This is an example of those who acquire the knowledge of the *Dīn* and benefit from that with which Allāh (T) sent me, and of those who do not take heed and who insist on rejecting Allāh's (T) Guidance.› [2]

The Messenger (S) likens the knowledge (with which he came) to rain, because both are causes of life. Rain is the cause of life for the body, while knowledge is the cause of life for the heart. He (S) also likens different hearts to different valleys, as Allāh (T) said:

﴿أَنزَلَ مِنَ ٱلسَّمَآءِ مَآءً فَسَالَتْ أَوْدِيَةٌۢ بِقَدَرِهَا﴾ الرعد ١٧

«He sends down water from the sky, making different valleys flow according to their different natures...» [3]

Thus, just as there are three kinds of land, there are three kinds of hearts:

1) The first is a good land which accepts water and is ready to

---

1 *Al-Jumuʿah* 62:5.

2 Al-Bukhārī and Muslim.

3 *Ar-Raʿd* 13:17.

produce vegetation. When rain falls on it, it absorbs the water eagerly, giving rise to all sorts of pleasant vegetation.

This is an example of one with a healthy, pure, and intelligent heart, which embraces knowledge, and is guided by its true intelligent nature, blossoming by that wisdom and true faith. Therefore, it is eager to take the knowledge, and ready to bear fruits because of its good nature.

It is also like a rich business man who has experience in different trades and investments, which enables him to invest his wealth in that which brings the best profit.

2) The second kind is a hard, solid land prepared to preserve and keep water: It benefits people who visit it to drink or irrigate.

This is an example of one whose heart preserves knowledge and safeguards it so as to convey it just as he hears it, without changing it or deriving conclusions from it. This is also described in another *hadīth*:

> **‹There is often one who conveys knowledge to one who is more knowledgeable than himself; and there is often one who carries knowledge when he himself is not knowledgeable.›** [1]

It is also like a rich man who does not possess the knowledge or experience to invest his wealth, but who knows very well how to preserve it.

3) The third is a barren land which is incapable of holding water or producing vegetation: no matter how much rain falls, it does not profit by it.

This is an example of one whose heart does not accept any knowledge or wisdom. It is also like a poor man who neither possesses wealth nor knows how to preserve it.

The first of the above three examples applies to a learned man who teaches knowledge, and who calls people to Allāh (T) with clear guidance; such are the inheritors of the Prophets.

The second applies to one who preserves the knowledge, and who transmits what he hears precisely; he carries to other people precious goods that they can use for trade and investment.

The third applies to one who neither accepts Allāh's Guidance nor

---

1 Narrated by Zayd bin Thābit, Anas bin Mālik and others; recorded by Abū Dāwūd, at-Tirmi<u>th</u>ī, Aḥmad, and others; authenticated by al-Albānī (*aṣ-Ṣaḥīḥah* no. 404).

benefits from it.

Thus this *ḥadīth* covers the different types of people and their different attitudes toward the Prophet's (S) *Da'wah*, which make them either happy or miserable.

The Second Class of Happy People

The second class of Happy People consists of the believers' followers from their offspring who die before reaching the status of *taklīf* [1]. They will be with their parents [in the Hereafter], as Allāh (T) said:

﴿وَٱلَّذِينَ آمَنُوا وَٱتَّبَعَتْهُمْ ذُرِّيَّتُهُمْ بِإِيمَانٍ أَلْحَقْنَا بِهِمْ ذُرِّيَّتَهُمْ وَمَا أَلَتْنَاهُمْ
مِنْ عَمَلِهِمْ مِنْ شَيْءٍ، كُلُّ آمْرِئٍ بِمَا كَسَبَ رَهِينٌ﴾ الطور ٢١

«As for those who believe and whose offspring follow them in faith, We shall unite them with their offspring, and We shall not let any of their deeds go to waste; every person is responsible for that which he has earned.» [2]

Allāh (T) tells that He unites the offspring with the parents in the *Jannah* [3], just as He united them in faith (*Īmān*). And because the offspring did not do deeds that would make them deserve this high honor, Allāh (T) informs that this union does not waste any of the deeds of the parents. They receive their full reward for what they did, plus the bonus of uniting them with their offspring.

Also, because this reunion in rewards and ranks is a bounty from Allāh (T), one might imagine that it would be in violation of the rules of justice. To clarify this, the *āyah* indicates that if the children committed sins, they alone would be liable for punishment, and that every person is responsible for what he does without involving others with him in punishment. Thus this union takes place in terms of rewards and bounties, but not in terms of justice and penalty.

This is indeed one of the keys and treasures of *Qur'ān*, the knowledge of which Allāh (T) gives only to those whom He wills.

Thus this *āyah* covers all people: the miserable and the happy - those who are followed, and those who follow them.

Consequently, let a prudent person who cares about his well-being

---

1 *Taklīf*: Responsibility for one's deeds.

2 *Aṭ-Ṭūr* 52:21.

3 *Jannah*: Literally: garden. It usually refers to the Gardens of Paradise.

see to which class he belongs. Let him not be influenced by habits or ruled by laziness. If he finds that he belongs to a happy class, let him strive to move to a higher rank, seeking Allāh's help and facilitation. And if he finds that he belongs to the miserable class, let him move out of it into a happy class while it is still possible, and before he would have to say:

﴿يَا لَيْتَنِي ٱتَّخَذْتُ مَعَ ٱلرَّسُولِ سَبِيلاً﴾ الفرقان ٢٧

«Oh! Would that I had followed the path shown to me by the Messenger.» [1]

1 *Al-Furqān* 25:27.

CHAPTER 8

REQUIREMENTS OF THE JOURNEY

One of the greatest forms of mutual help in righteousness and piety is to help one another in the journey of migration to Allāh and His Messenger (S). This help should be done by hands, tongues and hearts - through teaching, advising, educating, guiding, and caring.

If a person has this attitude toward Allāh's creatures, prosperity will rush to him from all directions, Allāh will move His creatures' hearts toward him, will open the gates of knowledge for his heart, and will facilitate the path of bliss for him.

Conversely, one with an opposite attitude will receive opposite consequences.

One might then ask, "You have described a very great journey and a very important matter; but what provisions should be taken along? Which way to follow? And what are the means to use for transportation?" The answer to this is provided in the following sections.

The Trip's Provisions

The provisions for this journey are the knowledge inherited from the Seal of Prophets (S) - there are no other provisions.

Let anyone not prepared with these provisions stay in his home and sit with those who lag behind. He would then find multitudes of other laggers to accompany. Let him follow their example; but let him know that this company will not avail him anything on the Day of Distress. Allāh (T) said:

﴿وَلَن يَنفَعَكُمُ ٱلْيَوْمَ إِذ ظَّلَمْتُمْ أَنَّكُمْ فِي ٱلْعَذَابِ مُشْتَرِكُونَ﴾ الزخرف ٣٩

«On that Day, it will avail you nothing that, since you have done wrong [together], you shall be partners in punishment [as well].» [1]

Thus Allāh (T) assures that the wrongdoers' association in punishment will not profit them. In this life, people find comfort in

1 *Az-Zukhruf* 43:39.

sharing disasters, as Al-Khansā'[2] said:

> "If it were not for the abundance of people wailing around me,
> Because of the loss of their brethren, I would have killed myself.
> And even though none of them wails the like of my brother, yet,
> I comfort myself in that we all share similar disasters."

However, this kind of consolation will not exist among those sharing the punishment on the Day of Resurrection.

The Way

The way to accomplish this journey is through exerting at full capacity and striving to the extreme. It can neither be accomplished by wishes, nor attained through loitering. It is only as a poet once said:

> "Dive into the darkness of death, and rise to eminence,
> Thus will you earn a distinguished and lasting honor.
> No good is in a soul that fears death,
> Nor in a willpower that worries about the reproachers' criticism."

It is not possible for a person to take this way unless one satisfies two matters:

1) First, as long as one is following the right way, one should never be concerned about the reproaches of those who like to find faults. Some types of reproach can hit even a strong knight so hard as to cause him to drop from his horse to the ground dead.

2) Second, one's soul should be so worthless to him, for Allāh's sake, that he would rush forward, fearless of any perils. The moment the soul becomes frightened, it retreats and turns away from facing dangers, preferring the lowliness of the earth.

These two matters cannot be further fulfilled without patience. One

---

1 An Arab poetess who lived in the time of *Jāhiliyyah* and in the early days of *Islām*.

who exercises patience for just a short while will find dangers turn into a smooth breeze which can carry him where he wishes. Thus the danger that he feared suddenly changes to become his best helper and assistant. This is a matter that cannot be comprehended well except by those who have tried it.

The Means of Ṭransportation

The means of transportation in this journey [of migration] is to take refuge in Allāh (T), and to turn to Him with one's whole being. It is to exhibit, by all means, full reliance on Him and true confidence in Him. It is to lie down before Him like a subdued and defeated person who possesses nothing - a person who looks up to his Master for dignity and security and for attaining some of His bounty, hoping that He would shelter him.

Such is the one whom, it is hoped, Allāh will guide and show what has been concealed from others concerning the way of this *hijrah* and its ranks.

Contemplating Allāh's *Āyāt*

The pinnacle of the whole affair [of performing a successful journey] and its central pillar is the continued contemplation on Allāh's *āyāt* - to such an extent that these *āyāt* would overpower the person's thoughts and fascinate his heart.

Once the meanings of the *Qur'ān* replace the passing thoughts of the heart - once the *Qur'ān* masters the person and controls his heart until he becomes its sole obeyed leader, then his journey goes smooth, and his course becomes manifest; and even when it appears to people that he is standing still, he would, in fact, be moving ahead so fast as to race with wind. [As Allāh (T) said:]

﴿وَتَرَى ٱلْجِبَالَ تَحْسَبُهَا جَامِدَةً وَهِيَ تَمُرُّ مَرَّ ٱلسَّحَابِ، صُنْعَ ٱللهِ ٱلَّذِي أَتْقَنَ كُلَّ شَيْءٍ، إِنَّهُ خَبِيرٌ بِمَا تَفْعَلُونَ﴾ النمل ٨٨

«You see the mountains and think them firmly fixed. But they pass away as the clouds pass away. [Such is] the mastery of Allāh who disposes of all things in perfect order. Indeed, He is well

acquainted with all that you do»[1]

One might ask, "You have pointed to a great aspiration. Would you disclose the door which opens into it; and would you raise the curtain that conceals it? Would you reveal how to understand thoroughly the meanings of the *Qur'ān*, and how to reflect upon its extraordinary delights and treasures? We have in our hands the books of *tafsīr* [2] of various *imāms*; are there any additional interpretations to be offered beyond what they have already done?"

I shall then present (in the next chapter) some examples that may be followed and taken as guide in this endeavor.

1 *An-Naml* 27:88.

2 *Tafsīr*: Explanation or interpretation. It frequently refers to volumes which include explanations and commentary of the *Qur'ān*.

CHAPTER 9

THOROUGH UNDERSTANDING OF THE *QUR'ĀN*

Magnificent Meanings in Ibrāhīm's Narration

Allāh (T) said:

﴿هَلْ أَتَاكَ حَدِيثُ ضَيْفِ إِبْرَاهِيمَ ٱلْمُكْرَمِينَ، إِذْ دَخَلُوا عَلَيْهِ فَقَالُوا: سَلَاماً، قَالَ: سَلَامٌ قَوْمٌ مُنْكَرُونَ. فَرَاغَ إِلَى أَهْلِهِ فَجَاءَ بِعِجْلٍ سَمِينٍ، فَقَرَّبَهُ إِلَيْهِمْ قَالَ: أَلَا تَأْكُلُونَ؟ فَأَوْجَسَ مِنْهُمْ خِيفَةً، قَالُوا: لَا تَخَفْ، وَبَشَّرُوهُ بِغُلَامٍ عَلِيمٍ. فَأَقْبَلَتِ ٱمْرَأَتُهُ فِي صَرَّةٍ، فَصَكَّتْ وَجْهَهَا وَقَالَتْ: عَجُوزٌ عَقِيمٌ. قَالُوا: كَذَٰلِكِ قَالَ رَبُّكِ، إِنَّهُ هُوَ ٱلْحَكِيمُ ٱلْعَلِيمُ. قَالَ: فَمَا خَطْبُكُمْ أَيُّهَا ٱلْمُرْسَلُونَ؟ قَالُوا: إِنَّا أُرْسِلْنَا إِلَى قَوْمٍ مُجْرِمِينَ، لِنُرْسِلَ عَلَيْهِمْ حِجَارَةً مِنْ طِينٍ، مُسَوَّمَةً عِنْدَ رَبِّكَ لِلْمُسْرِفِينَ. فَأَخْرَجْنَا مَنْ كَانَ فِيهَا مِنَ ٱلْمُؤْمِنِينَ، فَمَا وَجَدْنَا فِيهَا غَيْرَ بَيْتٍ مِنَ ٱلْمُسْلِمِينَ، وَتَرَكْنَا فِيهَا آيَةً لِلَّذِينَ يَخَافُونَ ٱلْعَذَابَ ٱلْأَلِيمَ﴾

الذاريات ٢٤-٣٧

«Has the story reached you of the honored guests of Ibrāhīm? That was when they entered his presence and said, "Peace [be upon you]!" He answered, "[And upon you be] peace, unfamiliar folks!" Then he turned quietly to his household, brought forth a fat [roasted] calf, and placed it before them. He said, "Will you not eat?" [When they did not reach for the meat] he conceived a fear of them; but they said, "Fear not," and gave him the glad tiding of [the birth of] a son who would be endowed with deep knowledge. Thereupon his wife came forward [laughing] aloud, and smote her face [in astonishment] and exclaimed: "A barren old woman [like me]!" They answered, "Thus has your Lord decreed; He is indeed the All-Wise and the All-Knower." [Ibrāmīm then] said: "And what else, [heavenly] messengers, is your errand?" They answered: "We have been sent to a people deep in sin, to launch clay stones on them, marked out in your Lord's

sight for [the punishment of] those who have wasted their own selves." And [in the course of time] We evacuated those of the believers who were there: For apart from a single house, We did not find there any *Muslims* [who had surrendered themselves to Us]. And so We left therein a message for those who fear the grievous suffering [which awaits all evildoers].»[1]

As one reads these *āyāt*, peering into their meanings and contemplating them, one gathers that the angels came to Ibrāhīm (S) in the form of guests who would normally eat and drink, that they announced to him the glad tiding of begetting a knowledgeable son, that his wife was astounded by the news, and that the angels told her that this was Allāh's command. One would possibly not perceive more than these meanings.

Let me then reveal just a few of the numerous marvels hidden in these *āyāt* - Let me demonstrate how they contain:

* high praise for Ibrāhīm,
* manners of hospitality,
* refutation of the dogmas of philosophers and *mu'aṭṭilah* [2],
* reference to Allāh's *ṣifāt*[3], particularly "Knowledge" and "Wisdom",
* brief and clear reference to the Resurrection, and to the certitude of its occurrence,
* description of the Lord's justice and His revenge against disbelieving nations,
* reference to *Islām* and *Īmān* and the difference between them,
* reference to the consistency of Allāh's signs which point to His *Tawhīd*, to the truthfulness of His messengers and to the Last Day, and
* that no one profits from all this except those whose hearts fear the punishment of the hereafter - those who believe in it; whereas no profit will reach those who do not fear it and who disbelieve in it.

I shall next present a detailed clarification of the preceding points.

---

1 *Ath-Thāriyāt* 51:24-37.

2 *Mu'aṭṭilah*: Those who deny the existence or reality of one or more of Allāh's attributes that appear in the *Qur'ān* and the *Ḥadīth*.

3 *Ṣifāt*: Plural of *ṣifah*, which means attribute. In the present context, it refers to Allāh's highest attributes.

Emphasis through Interrogation

Allāh (T) starts the narration with a question (**«Has the story reached you …?»**) that is not really intended as a query. Some scholars of the Arabic language assert that the question here means "indeed". Starting the discussion in situations like this with an interrogation carries a subtle message and an intricate meaning.

When a speaker wants to relate to the listeners an important matter requiring special emphasis, he would start with an interrogatory article to attract their attention. He would say for instance, "Did you know about such and such …?" Along this line, Allāh (T) said:

﴿هَلْ أَتَاكَ حَدِيثُ مُوسَىٰ﴾ طه ٩

«Has the story reached you of Mūsā?» [1]

And:

﴿وَهَلْ أَتَاكَ نَبَأُ ٱلْخَصْمِ﴾ ص ٢١

«Has the story reached you of the [two] disputants?» [2]

And:

﴿هَلْ أَتَاكَ حَدِيثُ ٱلْغَاشِيَةِ﴾ الغاشية ١

«Has there come unto you the tiding of the Overwhelming Event?» [3]

The purpose of the interrogation in all these *āyāt* is to emphasize the importance of the ensuing narrations, and to encourage pondering over them and comprehending the wisdom they carry.

It also serves another purpose: to remind that this knowledge is one of the clear signs of Muḥammad's prophethood: It belongs to the *ghayb* which neither he nor his people would have otherwise known about it. Did it reach him without Allāh's teaching and revelation? Did it come through any way other than Allāh's?

Glance then at this address appearing in the interrogatory form, and reflect over its great influence from all aspects. This would convince

---

1 *Ṭāhā* 20:9.

2 *Ṣād* 38:21.

3 *Al-Ghāshiyah* 88:1.

you that it is at the peak of eloquence.

High Praise for Ibrāhīm

HONORED GUESTS

The next words («... **the honored guests of Ibrāhīm** ...») carry a commendation by Allāh (T) for His *Khalīl* [1] Ibrāhīm. The word "honored" carries two meanings:

i) The first is that Ibrāhīm honored them, which is a compliment for his hospitality.

ii) The second is that they are honored by Allāh (T). This is similar to describing them elsewhere as «... **[The angels] are but His honored servants** ...» [2] This is another compliment for Ibrāhīm, because the honored angels were sent to visit him.

Thus both interpretations carry a praise for Ibrāhīm.

The next words («... **[they] said, "Peace [be upon you]!" He answered, "[And upon you be] peace"** ...») contain further praise for Ibrāhīm. He responded to the angels' greeting with a better one. Their greeting was "*Salāman*". This Arabic expression constitutes a verbal sentence [3] which, more precisely, means: "We greet you with peace." His response was "*Salāmun*". This is a nominal sentence which, more precisely, means: "Lasting and constant peace be on you." No doubt, the latter sentence implies constancy whereas the formal sentence implies change. Thus, Ibrāhīm's greeting was better and more complete.

---

1 *Khalīl*: A confidant and beloved friend. The *Qur'ān* declares that Allāh (T) has taken Ibrāhīm as His own *Khalīl* [*an-Nisā'* 4:125].

2 *Al-Anbiyā'* 21:26.

3 In Arabic, a sentence can either be verbal or nominal. A verbal sentence starts with a verb. Example: "The man came" would be expressed in Arabic as a verbal sentence: "Came the man". A nominal sentence, on the other hand, consists of nouns only (basically, two nouns: a *mubtada'* (starting noun or subject) and a *khabar* (describing noun)). Example: "The man is tall" would be expressed in Arabic as a nominal sentence: "The man tall", where "the man" is the *mubtada'* and "tall" is the *khabar*. In this sense, a verbal sentence describes a changing process (a process which took place at a certain time), whereas a nominal sentence describes a continuing process.

Manners in Criticism

The next words («... **unfamiliar folks!** ...») display two forms of good manners in addressing the guests, even when there is need to express concern because of their behavior:

i) He (S) dropped the subject of the sentence. Else, he would have said, "You are unfamiliar people." Thus he expressed concern without confronting them directly with it - which would be rude.

   This was also the manner of the Prophet Muḥammad (S) who, when criticizing some people's actions, instead of confronting them with what would hurt them, would rather say, **‹Why do some people do so and so ...?›**

ii) He (S) dropped mentioning the party affected by their unfamiliarity, namely, himself as stated elsewhere, «... **He deemed their conduct strange and became apprehensive of them** ...» [1] This is much more appropriate than saying, "You are unfamiliar to me."

Manners of Hospitality

In the next words («... **Then he turned quietly to his household** ...»), the verb used to describe Ibrāhīm's action is *rāgha*, which means "went quietly and secretly". This indicates his hastening to honor and serve his guests in a secret manner so that they would not feel shy.

This is to be contrasted with one who would purchase and prepare the food slowly and lazily, all in the presence of his guests. Such action would surely cause them to be bashful and disturbed.

Then the fact that he turned to no place other than his own household carries another compliment for Ibrāhīm (S). It indicates that all what is usually needed to honor and serve the guests is present and available within his household, without having to seek anything from the neighbors or elsewhere.

The next words («... **He brought forth a fat [roasted] calf** ...») contain three compliments for Ibrāhīm:

1. He served his guests personally rather then sending someone to serve them.

---

1 *Hūd* 11:70.

2. He brought before them a complete animal and not just a portion of it. This allows them to select any part of it that they would favor.
3. He did not bring before them a thin or lean animal, but rather a fat one. Being the young calf of a cow, this is further an expensive animal which would please the guests. His generosity and hospitality made him slaughter it despite its value.

The next words («… **and placed it before them** …») carry another compliment, because Ibrāhīm brought the food in front of the guests rather than putting it in another room and having them move to reach it.

The next words («… **He said, "Will you not eat?"** …») carry still another compliment for Ibrāhīm's fine manners of hospitality. Rather than saying, "Go ahead - eat!", he invited them to eat with these kind words, giving them the choice to eat or not.

Tiding of Isḥāq's Birth

It is commonly known that when the guests eat of their host's food, they please and pacify him. Thus when Ibrāhīm noticed that his guests did not reach for the meat, he conceived a fear in himself that they might have evil intentions.

When they perceived this they comforted him by revealing their identity, and they announced to him the news of the birth of a knowledgeable child («… **He conceived a fear of them; but they said, "Fear not," and gave him the glad tiding of [the birth of] a son who would be endowed with deep knowledge.** …»).

This child was Isḥāq, not Ismāʿīl, because his wife was surprised and mentioned that a barren old woman like herself cannot bear children. As for Ismāʿīl, he was his first-born child, and was born from his concubine Hājar. Allāh (T) clarified this in *sūrat Hūd*: **«We gave her the glad tiding of [the birth of] Isḥāq and, after Isḥāq, of [his son] Yaʿqūb.»** [1]

WOMEN'S NATURE

The next words («… **Thereupon his wife came forward [laughing]**

1 *Hūd* 11:71.

aloud, and smote her face [in astonishment] ...») display women's weakness and their emotional nature: as soon as she heard the news, she wailed and smote her face!

And then she «... **exclaimed: "A barren old woman [like me]!"** ...» This presents some of the good manners for a woman when talking to strangers. She would be brief and only use the words necessary to make herself clear. Thus Ibrāhīm's wife dropped the subject of the sentence which would otherwise be: "I am a barren woman," and she briefly mentioned what would prevent her from bearing children (old age). *Surat Hūd* [1] tells that she mentioned the reason preventing Ibrāhīm as well (old age too) from begetting children.

Wisdom, Knowledge and Other Attributes

The angels' reply («... **They answered, "Thus has your Lord spoken; He is indeed the All-Wise and the All-Knower."** ...») affirms the attributes of Speech for Allāh (T).

It also affirms Allāh s attributes of Wisdom (*al-Ḥakīm*) and Knowledge (*al-ʿAlīm*), which are the source of creation and decree. All of Allāh's creation, as well as His decree and law, result from His Knowledge and Wisdom.

Furthermore, Knowledge and Wisdom include all of Allāh's other Perfect Attributes.

Allāh's Perfect Knowledge implies His perfect Life (*al-Ḥayy*) and all that derives from it such as the Support for all the creation (*al-Qayyūm*), Power (*al-Qadīr*), Perseverance (*al-Bāqī*), Hearing (*as-Samīʿ*), and Seeing (*al-Baṣīr*).

His Perfect Wisdom implies perfect Will, Justice, Mercy, Benevolence, Generosity, and Kindness. It implies perfect judgement in doing things in the best possible way. It also implies justly decreeing and delivering rewards or punishment. All these meanings then derive from Allāh's (T) name: the All-Wise (*al-Ḥakīm*). The *Qurʾān* relates all these great matters to this attribute of Wisdom. It strongly rebukes those who claim that Allāh (T) created all the creation futilely and uselessly (without wisdom).

Because of this, it is most plausible to conclude that reason leads to the basic belief in the Resurrection, and that the Revelation comes with further confirmation and details of this belief.

The *Qurʾān*ic approach concerning Resurrection supports this conclusion. Allāh (T) gives two types of rational proofs concerning it:

---

1 *Hūd* 11:72.

1) The first type deals with the likelihood of its occurrence. Proofs for this derive from Allāh's Power.

2) The second type deals with the certitude of its occurrence. Proofs for this derive from Allāh's Wisdom.

One who examines these proofs will realize that they are quite sufficient and, praise be to Allāh (T), they leave no need for any other proofs. They are sound and satisfactory, they address the issue in a most direct way, and they include refutation and clarification of doubts and misconceptions that occur to many people.

If I be granted facilitation from Allāh (T), I shall write a large volume on this subject. I see that evidences presented in the *Qur'ān* carry cure, guidance, immediate clarification, clear expression, and warning and refutation of misconceptions. All this is presented in a way that pleases the heart and increases conviction, contrary to evidences from other sources. However, it is not possible to expound on this here.

What is meant then is that both Allāh's creation and His commands result from His Knowledge and Wisdom. This story specifically mentions these two attributes because people tend to be astonished when they hear of a baby being born for a couple who would not normally give birth. Thus there was need to point out that Allāh knows the reason and purpose of this creation, and that this decree conforms well with His Wisdom.

Destroying the People of Lūṭ

Next, Allāh (T) describes sending these angels to destroy Lūṭ's people by stoning them with marked stones («··· **[Ibrāmīm then] said: "And what else, [heavenly] messengers, is your errand?" They answered: "We have been sent to a people deep in sin, to launch clay stones on them, marked out in your Lord's sight for [the punishment of] those who have wasted their own selves."** ···»).

This shows that Allāh (T) supports His messengers and destroys their enemies. It points to the Resurrection, and it shows that rewards and punishment clearly take place in this world as well. This is one of the greatest proofs of the truthfulness of the messengers in delivering their Lord's Message.

Islām and *Īmān*

In the next words («··· **We evacuated those of the believers who were**

there: But We did not find there any except one *Muslim* household ···»), Allāh (T) makes a distinction between *Islām* (or *Muslims*) and *Īmān* (or believers). There is a subtle reason for this, which is called for because of the context.

The evacuation and deliverance from severe punishment was meant only for those believers who followed the messengers openly as well as secretly. This applied to only one household (that of Lūṭ), which could be described as a *Muslim* household.

Lūt's wife was a member of this household, and was apparently *Muslim*. But she was not to be among the rescued believers. Allāh (T) told about her betrayal of her husband, which was not in his honor, but in that she accepted her people's ways to such an extent that she went secretly to inform them about his guests. Thus she was apparently one of the *Muslim* household, but not one of the true believers who deserved to be rescued.

This answers a famous question: "Why is the more general term, *Islām,* excluded from the more specific term, *Īmān*? Does not the rule of exclusion require an opposite practice?" Based on the above discussion, it becomes clear that the "*Muslims*" are not excluded from the "believers" but from those who "were not found".

A Message for Those Who Fear

The last part («··· **and so We left therein a message for those who fear the grievous suffering [which awaits all evildoers].»**) points to Allāh's signs and marvels which He decreed in this world, and which He preserves as reminders of Himself and of the truthfulness of His messengers. These are beneficial only for those who believe in the Hereafter and fear Allāh's punishment. This is similar to what Allāh (T) said elsewhere:

﴿إِنَّ فِي ذَٰلِكَ لَآيَةً لِّمَنْ خَافَ عَذَابَ ٱلْآخِرَةِ﴾ هود ١٠٣

«Herein lies a message indeed for all who fear the punishment in the life to come.» [1]

And He said:

﴿سَيَذَّكَّرُ مَن يَخْشَىٰ﴾ الأعلى ١٠

«He will heed who fears [Allāh].» [2]

1 *Hūd* 11:103.

2 *Al-Aʿlā* 87:10.

As for those who do not believe in the Hereafter, when they see such signs they just say, "These are people who, like many others, were hit by misfortune. This is the norm of time: it gives happiness to some people and misfortune to others!"

But those who believe in the Hereafter and are afraid of it are the ones who benefit from these signs and reminders.

Conclusion

When a person understands the meanings and implications of the *Qur'ān* in the correct way, he will perceive marvels and wisdom that amaze the mind; and he will realize that it is indeed revealed by the All-Wise, the All-Benign.

This was meant to point out and to give examples as to how people vary in understanding the *Qur'ān* and in extracting its treasures and marvels. Indeed, bounties are in Allāh's hand and He gives of them to whom He wills.

CHAPTER 10
THE COMPANIONS IN THE ROAD

The Company of the Journey

When one sets his heart on taking this journey of migrating to Allāh (T) and His Messenger (S), one seeks a companion to befriend along the way. But one seldom finds such a companion. All what one finds are:

i) those who contradict and oppose him,

ii) those who constantly blame and frankly rebuke him,

iii) or those who avoid him, having absolutely no inclination to consider such a trip.

I wish that all people were of this last type: he would indeed be kind to you who avoids you and who does not inflict his harms on you. A poet once said:

> "We are in a time when refraining from evil is viewed,
> by most people, as an act of bounty and kindness."

With this being the common practice of people, what is required today from them is to help in this journey by avoiding blame and opposition, except to those who drop out along the road.

One should not rely in his trip on such dropouts, but should move along, even if one had to be a lone stranger. Pursuing this journey without company would then constitute a strong proof of the truthfulness of one's love (to Allāh (T) and His Messenger (S)).

The Living and the Dead

He who intends to undertake this journey should accompany the dead who are in reality alive [1] (because of their lasting knowledge and bounties among people); their company will enable him to reach his

1 This company is a spiritual one, whereby a person tries to learn about and adhere to the way of the *Ṣaḥābah* and the early people of piety and knowledge.

goal. And he should avoid the company of the living people who are in reality dead; they would disrupt his way.[1]

Nothing is more important to the traveler than to associate with the first [living] company, and to disown the second [dead] company. One of the *Salaf* said:

> "The difference is indeed great between those who are dead - but whose remembrance brings life to the hearts, and those who are alive - but whose company causes death to the hearts."

Thus, nothing is more harmful for a person than his peers and associates. His eyesight and his aspirations are usually limited to imitating them, boasting to them, and following their footsteps; even if they entered into the hole of a lizard, he would love to enter with them.

Good Manners in Dealing with the Ignorant

After a person turns away from the company of those [ignorant associates], and he turns to the company of those who are absent in person - but whose bounties and good influence continue to exist in the world, he would then acquire a new zeal and a new direction, and he would become a stranger among the people - even if he be a relative or a close acquaintance.

This would make him a dear stranger to people. He can clearly see the obscurity that they suffer, but they cannot see the splendor which he enjoys. He excuses them as much as he can, while enjoining and advising them to do good with all of his power. Thus he looks at them with two eyes:

a) With one eye, he recognizes Allāh's commands and prohibitions. Based of this, he advises or warns them, and befriends or disowns them, giving them their rights and requiring his.

b) With the other eye, he recognizes Allāh's Decree and Measure. Based of this, he sympathizes with them; he makes *du'ā* (supplications) for them; he asks Allāh (T) to forgive them;

1 This may not be understood as a call to monkshood and seclusion. It is merely an advice to avoid getting so much immersed in the futile pastimes of people as to become diverted from the more important mission of migration to Allāh (T) and His Messenger (S).

and he seeks excuses for them in matters that do not involve violation of Allāh's commands and His *Shar'*[1]. He engulfs them with kindness, compassion and forgiveness, heeding to Allāh's command [to His Messenger (S)]:

﴿خُذِ ٱلْعَفْوَ، وَأْمُرْ بِٱلْعُرْفِ، وَأَعْرِضْ عَنِ ٱلْجَاهِلِينَ﴾ الأعراف ١٩٩

«Show forgiveness, enjoin what is good, and turn away from the foolish» [2]

If a person abides by this *āyah*, it would suffice and cure him. It calls for:

a) Good manners in dealing with people: by forgiving them and showing them compassion to the limits of one's character and nature.

b) Fulfilling Allāh's rights in people by enjoining what is good, which applies to matters that the minds attest to their goodness and merit, based on what Allāh has commanded.

c) Avoiding their evil: to ward off the harm resulting from their ignorance, without trying to avenge himself.

How else can a person attain perfection? And what policy and behavior can be better in this world than this? If a man tries to consider every evil reaching him from people (I mean a true evil that results in a loss of honor before Allāh (T)), he will find that it arises from neglecting one or more of these three matters. If he abides by them all, then whatever is inflicted on him by people will be good, even if it appears to be evil. Only good can result from enjoining good, even if it be encased in a situation of evil and harm. Allāh (T) said:

﴿إِنَّ ٱلَّذِينَ جَاءُوا بِٱلْإِفْكِ عُصْبَةٌ مِنْكُمْ، لَا تَحْسَبُوهُ شَرًّا لَكُمْ، بَلْ هُوَ خَيْرٌ لَكُمْ﴾ النور ١١

«Verily! Those who brought forth the great slander [against 'Ā'ishah (R)] are a group among you. Consider it not a bad thing for you. Nay, it is good for you.» [3]

---

1 *Shar'*: Allāh's Divine Law.

2 *Al-A'rāf* 7:199.

3 *An-Nūr* 24:11.

And He addressed His Messenger (S) by saying:

﴿فَاعْفُ عَنْهُمْ وَاسْتَغْفِرْ لَهُمْ وَشَاوِرْهُمْ فِي الْأَمْرِ فَإِذَا عَزَمْتَ فَتَوَكَّلْ عَلَى اللَّهِ﴾ آل عمران ١٥٩

«So forgive them, ask Allāh to forgive them, and consult them in the affair. Then when you have taken a decision, put your full trust in Allāh.» [1]

This *āyah* instructs the Messenger (S) to fulfill Allāh's rights and the people's rights. When people do wrong, they would either be violating Allāh's limits or harming His Messenger personally. If they harm the Messenger (S), he should respond by forgiving them. But if they overstep Allāh's limits, then he (S) should ask Allāh (T) to forgive them and to soften their hearts. Also, he (S) should extract their opinions by consulting them, because this tends to make them more obedient and willing to advise. Once he forms his decision, he should seek advice no more, but should rather put his trust in Allāh and go forth to fulfill what he decided, for Allāh loves those who trust Him.

Three Conditions to Acquire Excellent Manners

This is one example of the excellent manners with which Allāh (T) has equipped his Messenger (S). He described him as:

﴿وَإِنَّكَ لَعَلَى خُلُقٍ عَظِيمٍ﴾ القلم ٤

«Verily, You [Muḥammad] are on an exalted standard of character.»[2]

'Ā'ishah (R) described him as:

> "His character was just [a reflection of] the *Qur'an*." [3]

Such excellent character cannot be attained without three conditions:

1. The foundation must be good. If one has a rough and dry nature, it will be hard for him to submit to this [excellence of character]

---

1 *Āl-'Imrān* 3:159.

2 *Al-Qalam* 68:4.

3 Recorded by Muslim, Abū Dāwūd, and Aḥmad.

through knowledge, will, or practice. On the other hand, a mild and smooth nature will be ready and willing to receive the plowing and the seeds [to prepare it for character excellence].

2. The soul must be strong and capable of conquering calls of laziness, transgression, and desire. These matters contradict perfection, and souls which cannot defeat them will always be defeated and conquered.

3. [One must possess] a discerning knowledge of the truth of matters, enabling one to put them in the rightful position, and to distinguish between flesh and cancer - between glass and jewels.

If these three qualities are present in a man, and Allāh's facilitation helps him, then he will be among those to whom the best (*ḥusnā*) has been decreed and for whom Allāh's care has been secured.

A Gift for the Lovers of Allāh and His the Messenger

If you peer into the words contained in these leaflets, you will perceive that they describe what is most required for mutual help in *birr* and *taqwā*, and in migrating to Allāh and His Messenger. This is what the author intended when he wrote this treatise, making it an early and expedited gift to his friends and companions in seeking the knowledge.

Allāh is the witness, **«and Allāh is sufficient as a Witness»** [1], that if this treatise reaches any of such friends, he will meet it with acceptance, and will hasten to understand it, and will consider it as one of the best possible gifts among friends. Other types of [material] bountiful gifts, even if people look forward to them, have little benefits and are extremely trivial because too many people can give them. Indeed, a useful gift is a [good] word that a man presents to his *Muslim* brother.

Allāh (T) indeed knows best.

[In conclusion,] may Allāh (T) bestow His praise and blessings and perfect peace on our Prophet Muḥammad and his family and companions, until the Day of Judgement. And, *al-ḥamdu li 'Llāhi rabb il ʿālamīn*.

---

1 *An-Nisāʾ* 4:79, and several other places in the *Qurʾān*.

INDEX OF ARABIC TERMS

AL-QUR'ĀN WAS-SUNNAH SOCIETY
OF NORTH AMERICA

Al-Qur'ān was-Sunnah Society is distinguished by its clear and firm methodology (the Methodology of the *salaf*) that centers around:

a) *Tawḥīd*,
b) adherence to the *Qur'ān* and *Sunnah*, and
c) following the Guidance of the *Salaf* (the Companions of the Prophet (S) and their true followers).

The main goal of the Society is to return to *Islām*, understand it, practice it, and call to it, in accordance with the Methodology of the *salaf*.

In order to realize this, the Society attempts to cooperate with Muslim individuals and organizations that belong to *Ahl us-Sunnati wal-Jamā'ah*, and present *Islām*, pure and clear, to non-Muslims, and invite them to it.

Al-Qur'ān was-Sunnah Society emphasizes mature work, abandoning all forms of *'aṣabiyyah* (factionism), and honoring the *'Ulamā* (learned scholars of *Islām*).

We asks Allāh (T) to grant us truthfulness, sincerity, and perseverance in obeying Him. If this be granted, then we are certain of His help and support, because there is no true help and support except His.

1526 S. Center St. • Arlington, TX 76010, USA • ✆ 817-548-3134 • FAX: 817-548-3135